NEW TESTAMENT MESSAGE

A Biblical-Theological Commentary

Wilfrid Harrington, O.P. and Donald Senior, C.P.

EDITORS

New Testament Message, Volume 18

HEBREWS

Juliana Casey, I.H.M.

VERITAS PUBLICATIONS/DUBLIN

2

Published by
VERITAS PUBLICATIONS
7-8 Lower Abbey Street, Dublin

in cooperation with

MICHAEL GLAZIER, INC.
Wilmington, Delaware

227.87 E
CASE

International Standard Book Number 0-86217-033-8

Printed in the United States of America by Abbey Press

CONTENTS

EDITORS' PREFACE

New Testament Message is a commentary series designed to bring the best of biblical scholarship to a wide audience. Anyone who is sensitive to the mood of the church today is aware of a deep craving for the Word of God. This interest in reading and praying the scriptures is not confined to a religious elite. The desire to strengthen one's faith and to mature in prayer has brought Christians of all types and all ages to discover the beauty of the biblical message. Our age has also been heir to an avalanche of biblical scholarship. Recent archaeological finds, new manuscript evidence, and the increasing volume of specialized studies on the Bible have made possible a much more profound penetration of the biblical message. But the flood of information and its technical nature keeps much of this scholarship out of the hands of the Christian who is eager to learn but is not a specialist. *New Testament Message* is a response to this need.

The subtitle of the series is significant: "A Biblical-Theological Commentary." Each volume in the series, while drawing on up-to-date scholarship, concentrates on bringing to the fore in understandable terms the specific message of each biblical author. The essay-format (rather than a word-by-word commentary) helps the reader savor the beauty and power of the biblical message and, at the same time, understand the sensitive task of responsible biblical interpretation.

A distinctive feature of the series is the amount of space given to the "neglected" New Testament writings, such as Colossians, James, Jude, the Pastoral Letters, the Letters of Peter and John. These briefer biblical books make a significant but often overlooked contribution to the richness of the New Testament. By assigning larger than normal coverage to these books, the series hopes to give these parts of Scripture the attention they deserve.

Because *New Testament Message* is aimed at the entire English speaking world, it is a collaborative effort of international proportions. The twenty-two contributors represent biblical scholarship in North America, Britain, Ireland and Australia. Each of the contributors is a recognized expert in his or her field, has published widely, and has been chosen because of a proven ability to communicate at a popular level. And, while all of the contributors are Roman Catholic, their work is addressed to the Christian community as a whole. The New Testament is the patrimony of all Christians.It is the hope of all concerned with this series that it will bring a fuller appreciation of God's saving Word to his people.

Wilfrid Harrington, O.P.
Donald Senior, C.P.

To the IHM sisters, my co-ministers, and especially—right here and right now—to Mary Ann and Dorothy.

"Let us go forth unto Him." Hebrews 13:13

INTRODUCTION

EVERY ONCE IN A WHILE we read something, or hear something, which appeals to us, which seems to speak to an unspoken need deep in our hearts. Sometimes we sense that there is even more in this mysterious saying, if only we could truly understand it. All Scripture is like this. As God's word, it is filled with healing and hope, call and challenge; it speaks to our heart and places our human situation in a different perspective. At the same time, it always remains a mystery to us; its depth can never be plumbed, nor its richness exhausted.

God's word in Scripture is also the human word. Written by real people in real situations, it carries with it the vagaries of socially conditioned human expression. Frequently that human expression, so removed as it is from our own way of speaking, acts as a veil which shrouds the richness of the message and impedes our understanding. We find ourselves before the word, sensing the treasure that is there yet unable to grasp it.

Nowhere is this more true than with the "Epistle to the Hebrews." One of the most compelling statements of the meaning of Jesus the Christ and of the gift and challenge that is the Christian life, Hebrews remains clouded in a language that is nearly incomprehensible to contemporary men and women. This text has always been a mystery, and has occasioned great debates throughout the history of its interpretation. Very little agreement exists concerning most points of Hebrews.

xii

The Community

Disagreement begins with the title itself. The title "To the Hebrews" was not an original part of the text, but was added sometime in the fourth century. There is, therefore, no agreement about the nature of the community which received Hebrews. Were they Gentile Christians, Jewish Christians, unconverted persons? Were they in Jerusalem, in Rome, or somewhere else? All of these have been suggested and all are possible. There are some clues to the identity of the "Hebrews" within the text itself. There are indications (Heb 10:32-34; 12:4) that the community was in trouble and had known some form of persecution. We also know they were not eyewitnesses of the Jesus-event, but had heard of him from others (Heb 2:3). Hebrews develops its major themes against a background of old covenant institutions such as the Levitical priesthood, the ceremonies of the Day of Atonement, the construction of the sacred tent of the days of the exodus. In contrast to these, the new priesthood of Jesus, the final atonement, the holy city of the new covenant are presented. Since the author presumes an in-depth knowledge of the old covenant institutions, we may assume that members of the community were Jewish Christians imbued with knowledge of and love for their Judaic heritage.

Authorship

The person responsible for the "Epistle to the Hebrews" was also very well acquainted with the Judaic tradition. The many, many quotations from the Old Testament as well as the frequent references to the old covenant institutions make this clear. At the same time, the author knew Greek very well. Hebrews contains some of the most highly-developed Greek in the New Testament. He also knew Greek thought and sometimes inserted technical terms such as "shadow" (8:5; 10:1), and "copy" (8:5; 9:23). These terms, and their use to suggest a dualism which posited a dichotomy between heavenly reality and its lesser shadow (the earthly counterpart), lead one to recognize that in Hebrews we meet a unique combination of two major trends of thought: the Judaic and the more philosophical Greek.

There is no certainty as to the identity of the person so knowledgeable of both traditions, so gifted in his use of the Greek language. There is general agreement that the author is not Paul. Too many differences between Hebrews and the Pauline epistles exist for us to say they were written by the same person. The names most frequently mentioned are Barnabas, the "son of encouragement" (Acts 4:36), Apollos, "a man of eloquence" (Acts 18:24-28), Priscilla, who, according to Acts 18:26, was Apollos' teacher. There are serious reasons why none of these three are certain, however. All we can know for sure is that Hebrews comes to us from a person who is extremely gifted, very knowledgeable and filled with a profoundly intense concern about the community.

Hebrews: A Homily

The intensity and urgency of Hebrews have led scholars to an important conclusion. The "Epistle to the Hebrews" is not an epistle. If one compares the beginning of Hebrews with the other epistles the differences are striking. The names of the author and the community, the greeting, the personal information given at the opening of the epistles (see, for example, 1 Cor 1:1-17) are all missing in Hebrews. Further, the emphasis in Hebrews is always on the *spoken* word, not the written. The only verses which resemble an epistle are found at the very end of Hebrews (13:19, 22-25) and were probably added at a later date.

The Epistle to the Hebrews is really a homily first delivered orally and then sent to other communities for their encouragement. This is an important fact for it affects the way we understand Hebrews. We must listen to it rather than read it. We must place ourselves among the community to whom this homily was spoken. This implies a greater involvement and a stronger sense of being addressed directly. The urgency of Hebrews becomes more understandable to us when we realize that its "author" is in fact a preacher whose aim is to move his community to conversion and to fidelity. As we listen to Hebrews, the lengths to which the preacher will go in order to attain his goal become *very* evident.

The Message

The reason for the extreme urgency of our preacher is made clear when we turn to the message that Hebrews speaks. That message contains two elements: the meaning of the Christ-event; the consequences of that event for the believer. The meaning of the Christ-event lies in the fact that in Jesus' sacrifice sin has finally been forgiven. Because Jesus effected this in his gift of himself in death, the believer can now approach God. The barrier of sin which stood between God and his people has been destroyed. The homilist views all of the history of the old covenant as continued attempts to attain forgiveness of sin, continued *futile* attempts. The law, the cult, the sacrifices of the Old Testament are all shown to be ineffectual in order that the greatness of Jesus' sacrifice might be revealed in all its grace. In Jesus, God has once-for-all forgiven our sin.

This fact has enormous consequences for the believer. In the first place, it is the ground for great hope and confidence. One need no longer fear, for Jesus has saved us and continues to intercede for us. We can be *sure* that true relationship to God is possible for us. Secondly, the believer must leave the past behind and move forward in faith in Jesus, the Son of God. The "Hebrews" are a discouraged people who have grown weary with the life that is theirs. They are also a "homesick" people who long for the rich life they knew as people of the old covenant. They are tempted to give up the struggle and to go back to their former allegiance.

In face of this temptation, the homilist repeatedly urges them to hold fast to what they have been given. He continuously refers to the richest elements of their former life in order show that while profoundly beautiful, they did not work. Imperfect as they were, they served to point toward a future, perfect covenant. This new covenant has become a reality in Jesus. Would they give up the perfect for the sake of a faulty, ineffectual old covenant? Would they refuse their inheritance?

If they did, there would be no way out. They were condemned. The homilist considers the danger of apostasy to be so grave that he paints a gruesome picture of what lies in store for the apostate. There is no hope for those who give up, who knowingly reject what is theirs.

Hebrews Today

What has this mysterious homily filled with irrelevant images and warnings about apostasy to do with us? *We* are not tempted to return to the religious life of the Old Testament; *we* are not contemplating apostasy. Perhaps we should simply admire Hebrews for the literary masterpiece that it is and value it for the insight it offers into life in an early christian community. Perhaps we should admit that this strange (and strangely beautiful) homily preached to an unknown community by an unknown preacher is really not significant for us today.

However, the message of Hebrews is *very* pertinent today in ways that challenge the very fabric of our lives as Christians. The message that sin is forgiven has yet to be really believed. We live in a world where all morality seems to have disappeared, where law no longer binds or constrains us. We have, it seems, denied the very existence of sin. And yet we are very, very uncomfortable in this "sinless" world of ours. Deep in our hearts most of us suspect that we are indeed sinners and that we will have to pay in the end. We are a guilty world and sometimes we seem to glory in our guilt. We boast of our freedom and yet are slaves to the very sin we deny.

Hebrews has something important to say to this. Sin is *forgiven*, not denied. The homilist makes no attempt to deny the reality that is sin; he is very conscious of it and of what it does to the human heart. His point is precisely here: our sense of guilt and constant denials are no longer necessary. This is so because God has done what we could not do, he has forgiven. We are free now, truly free to live without fear, to approach our God who is loving, compassionate, merciful. God does not make us pay, he forgives – if we allow it.

Hebrews is about Jesus, the Christ. It gives us a brother who has fully shared in our human existence, who is not ashamed of us, who knows what it is to be human. This brother has saved us, has enabled us to live in confidence without fear. Hebrews also tells us that Jesus lives now. Alive with the Father, he continues to intercede for us and to welcome us. He continues to say to us, "You are forgiven, you belong here."

The challenge is ours. Can we really believe that God forgives? Can we allow him to be God and do what we cannot do? Are we able to believe and to live freely in the hope and confidence that has been given us?

Can we go forward? At first sight, this question seems absurd in our constantly changing world. We have known more change, more advance than perhaps any other period in history. Our technology has made the world a village, our knowledge has expanded immeasurably, our religious institutions have changed drastically in the past fifteen years. All of these advances have provoked a sense of terror within us. Technology has created a world where computers rule our lives and nuclear arms stand ready to destroy us. Knowledge has led to repeated revolutions and to a terrorism that can hold the whole world as hostage. Religious changes have provoked unrest, dissatisfaction and deep divisions among us.

We are, I think, afraid of what we have created, and we are afraid of our future. A recent survey of young people in the United States is very telling. When asked the same questions posed to young people in the 1950's, today's youth revealed that they were much less hopeful, were actually pessimistic about the future. They did not feel their lives would improve in the next twenty years. In reaction to this fear there is a growing inclination to stop, to retrench, to return to the security of the past. Life has never been more of a risk, and we don't like it. We want to exchange our new, as yet unwritten dictionaries for older editions where all the words are familiar. We want to go back, we're lonely for the security of our past.

So were the "Hebrews." Their lives as Christians were unfamiliar to them *and* risky. To them our homilist cried, "Look to Jesus, go forward with him!" The message of forgiveness, the call to courage and to hope, the challenge to risk are desperately needed today; and God's word, alive and active in Hebrews, is gift to us.

A Note About Language:

In this community the homilist is consistently referred to as "he." This is so because the evidence for male authorship (either Barnabas or Apollos) seems stronger than for a female author (Priscilla, for example). The use of the masculine in no way implies that a woman could not have written Hebrews or that women were not preachers in the early communities.

INTRODUCTION:
GOD HAS SPOKEN IN A SON.
1:1-4.

1 In many and various ways God spoke of old to our fathers by the prophets; ²but in these last days he has spoken to us by a Son, whom he appointed the heir of all things, through whom also he created the world. ³He reflects the glory of God and bears the very stamp of his nature, upholding the universe by his word of power. When he had made purification for sins, he sat down at the right hand of the Majesty on high, ⁴having become as much superior to angels as the name he has obtained is more excellent than theirs.

These four introductory verses give ample evidence of the masterful language and exalted tone which characterize Hebrews. All four verses are one sentence in the original language which flow smoothly along until they reach the final word (name) which in turn becomes the subject of the next section (1:5-2:18). These introductory verses, which stress the word of God and God's activity of speaking (vs. 1: God spoke; vs. 2: he has spoken; vs. 3: upholding the universe by his *word* of power), differ radically from the introduction to any epistle that we have in the New Testament. Here we have no name, no address to a particular community, no greetings at all, in fact. Instead we are confronted with an eloquent statement of what God has done in his Son. The oratorical style, with its stress on the spoken word, will continue throughout the homily that we know as "The Epistle to the Hebrews."

The homilist employs his style to its full measure to introduce what will become major themes of Hebrews, all of these radiate from that which is central: the Son of God. First, we are told that the multiple revelations of the old covenant have been surpassed for now God has spoken in a Son. Implied here is a comparison which will appear again and again in Hebrews: the multiplicity and repetition of the old covenant realities in face of the uniqueness and efficacy of the new. Further, the homilist proclaims that, with the revelation in the Son, the new eschatological age (*in these last days*) has begun. Thus, the "Hebrews" live now in the eschatological age. This fact becomes very important when the speaker turns to the community in exhortation.

But who is this one in whom eschatological revelation has been spoken? The homilist provides seven definitions, most of which (in images reminiscent of Jn 1:1-18) stress the greatness of the Son, his closeness to the Father, his power. This one is Son, he is the exalted one who is now at the right of the majesty on high. Both the idea of sonship and of exaltation play very significant roles in Hebrews, as we shall see. There is yet another phrase here, one often overlooked in the grandeur of these descriptions, yet one which perhaps plays the most important role in Hebrews' understanding of the significance of the Son: he achieved purification of sin. This phrase, which sums up the earthly ministry of the Son, introduces what to our homilist is the crucial issue at stake in his homily: in the Son and *only* in the Son was sin forgiven. It is this fact which makes possible the boundless encouragement and dire warnings with which the Hebrews must be faced.

It is this achievement, we are told, which led to the exaltation of the Son and which made him superior to the angels as his name is superior to any other name. The superiority spoken of here is not only of quality (as when brand X is better than brand Y) but implies superiority of a whole different *kind.* The Son is better than the angels, his name is more excellent because he is, in his very nature, *different* from the angels.

I. JESUS: EXALTED SON, COMPASSIONATE BROTHER. 1:5 – 2:18

These first two chapters reveal one of the most striking characteristics of Hebrews: the combination of seeming opposites. We are introduced to one of the most lofty presentations of the exalted Son of God in the New Testament and to one of the most graphic descriptions of Jesus— truly human, truly brother.

THE SON—GREATER THAN THE ANGELS. 1:5-14.

> 5For to what angel did God ever say,
> "Thou art my Son,
> today I have begotten thee"?
> Or again,
> "I will be to him a father,
> and he shall be to me a son"?
> 6And again, when he brings the firstborn into the world,
> he says,
> "Let all God's angels worship him."
> 7Of the angels he says,
> "Who makes his angels winds,
> and his servants flames of fire."
> 8But of the Son he says,
> "Thy throne, O God, is for ever
> and ever,

the righteous scepter is the scepter
of thy kingdom.
⁹Thou hast loved righteousness and
hated lawlessness;
therefore God, thy God, has
anointed thee
with the oil of gladness beyond thy
comrades."
¹⁰And,
"Thou, Lord, didst found the earth
in the beginning,
and the heavens are the work of
thy hands;
¹¹they will perish, but thou
remainest;
they will all grow old like a garment,
¹²like a mantle thou wilt roll them up,
and they will be changed.
But thou art the same,
and thy years will never end."
¹³But to what angel has he ever said,
"Sit at my right hand,
till I make thy enemies
a stool for thy feet"?
¹⁴Are they not all ministering spirits sent forth to serve,
for the sake of those who are to obtain salvation?

The homilist now proceeds to develop the topic suggested
in verse 4: the Son is superior in every way to the angels.
Concerned, perhaps, that the community has a tendency
towards angel worship (a phenomenon not unheard of in
early Christianity), he presents them with indisputable
proof that the Son is more excellent in that he is Son, whom
angels worship. His powers are immeasurably greater and
he is seated at the right hand of God.

A characteristic method of argument is demonstrated
here for the first time. A whole series of Old Testament

quotations (which the author sees as God's word) are given and applied to Son and angels respectively. It is the very Scriptures themselves which prove our homilist's point! Thus, Psalm 2:7, (Thou art my son. . .), we are told, is addressed by God to the Son *only* and not to angels, as is 2 Sam 7:14 (I will be to him a father. . .).

The angels are to worship this Son, this first-born of God (Dt 32:43). The angels of God are spirits and ministers (Ps 104:4), they are *not* the Son. The Son, further, is an enthroned one who has been anointed by God and placed above all others (Ps 45:6-7). He is also Lord, who creates and who remains the same though all creation shall perish (Ps 102:25-27). Finally, the Son is called to the right hand of God where he remains until the final consummation (Ps 110:1), while the angels are sent forth to minister to those who will inherit salvation.

The homilist, then, uses seven citations to establish that the *one* Son is more than and different from the many angels. He also introduces further terms and texts which will play significant roles in later sections of Hebrews. In verse 6 he establishes the fact that Jesus is the first-born. In a culture where the first-born has special significance, particularly in terms of inheritance, this designation is very important. Our homilist will eventually extend this term and apply it to the Christians, thus evoking their relationship to the one Son and to their sharing in his inheritance. Further, reference to the Son at the right hand of God is a clear indication that Hebrews contains an *exaltation* Christology; that is, an understanding of Christ which saw beyond the Resurrection to the enthronement of Christ in the heavens. This development in Christological understanding was a natural one, but one which developed after a period of reflection, reflection which probably began with an understanding of Jesus as the suffering servant spoken of by Isaiah, and which eventually recognized the great Old Testament texts about an enthroned one as descriptions of the Risen, Exalted Christ.

Finally, the homilist cites one of *the* great texts of exaltation, Psalm 110, which appears over thirty times in the
New Testament. The Psalm is an important one for him,
not only in terms of exaltation of the Son but also because
Psalm 110:4 refers to the high priesthood of Melchizedek,
an idea that becomes *very* significant in Chapter 5.

LISTEN CAREFULLY.
2:1-4.

> **2** Therefore we must pay the closer attention to what
> we have heard, lest we drift away from it. ²For if the
> message declared by angels was valid and every trans-
> gression or disobedience received a just retribution,
> ³how shall we escape if we neglect such a great salvation?
> It was declared at first by the Lord, and it was attested
> to us by those who heard him, ⁴while God also bore
> witness by signs and wonders and various miracles and
> by gifts of the Holy Spirit distributed according to his
> own will.

In 2:1-4 the homilist involves the hearers for the first
time. Building upon what has been established concerning
the superiority of the Son over the angels, the homilist
stresses the importance of the word spoken by that Son as
compared to the word spoken by the angels.

If the angels' word carries a retribution for those who did
not heed it, how much more shall rejection of the much
greater word of the Son carry retribution? The homilist
introduces the first in a series of exhortations, all of which
give a great sense of urgency to Hebrews. They all contain
a two-pronged theme: there is danger in neglecting the salvation made available in Jesus Christ; a sure and disastrous
fate awaits those who do turn from this salvation.

These few verses also introduce us to a very important
stylistic characteristic of Hebrews and one which points
to the difference between Hebrews and the Pauline epistles:

the constant alternation of *genre*. Whereas Paul frequently writes an extensive section wherein he exposes a principal idea and then appends an exhortation, the homilist consistently weaves both exposition and exhortation together throughout the entire homily. This type of alternation is more in keeping with what we would expect from a homily which must constantly involve the hearers and move them in fear and in hope. Once again here we see the stress on the *spoken* word, spoken by angels, and the Son. The Son's word was borne witness to by God himself and confirmed by those who heard him speak.

The reference to those who heard the Son speak is one of the few indications given to us as to the background of the community of "Hebrews." Neither the homilist nor the community were eyewitnesses to the Christ-event, but rather had heard of it from others who were. This fact can indicate two things. The "Hebrews" were second generation Christians and their community came into existence after the death of the eyewitnesses, or they were "diaspora" Christians who were physically removed from Jerusalem and the area of Christ's ministry. Whichever is the case, we know that they were a community which grounded their faith upon the message proclaimed by those who had seen and who had heard the Lord directly.

JESUS, MADE PERFECT THROUGH SUFFERING. 2:5-18.

> [5]For it was not to angels that God subjected the world to come, of which we are speaking. [6]It has been testified somewhere,
>> "What is man that thou art mindful of him,
>> or the son of man, that thou carest for him?
>> [7]Thou didst make him for a little while lower than
>>   the angels,
>> thou has crowned him with glory and honor,
>> [8]putting everything in subjection under his feet."

Now in putting everything in subjection to him, he left nothing outside his control. As it is, we do not yet see everything in subjection to him. [9]But we see Jesus, who for a little while was made lower than the angels, crowned with glory and honor because of the suffering of death, so that by the grace of God he might taste death for every one.

[10]For it was fitting that he, for whom and by whom all things exist, in bringing many sons to glory, should make the pioneer of their salvation perfect through suffering. [11]For he who sanctifies and those who are sanctified have all one origin. That is why he is not ashamed to call them brethren, [12]saying,

"I will proclaim thy name to my brethren,
in the midst of the congregation I will praise thee."
[13]And again,

"I will put my trust in him."
And again,
"Here am I, and the children God has given me."
[14]Since therefore the children share in flesh and blood, he himself likewise partook of the same nature, that through death he might destroy him who has the power of death, that is, the devil, [15]and deliver all those who through fear of death were subject to lifelong bondage. [16]For surely it is not with angels that he is concerned but with the descendants of Abraham. [17]Therefore he had to be made like his brethren in every respect, so that he might become a merciful and faithful high priest in the service of God, to make expiation for the sins of the people. [18]For because he himself has suffered and been tempted, he is able to help those who are tempted.

The tone changes in the rest of chapter 2 as the homilist turns to the redemption effected by the Son and to his solidarity with humankind. After the suggestion of frightening consequences in 2:1-4, we are now given much cause for consolation.

In the first section of this text (vss. 5-9) once again an Old Testament quotation (Ps 8:4-6) serves as a basis for pointing to the supremacy of the Son over all creation. This citation suggests not only the exaltation of the Son but also his humiliation. While there is nothing not under his control, he is also the one who has been made lower than the angels. This reference to the humiliation of the Son of Man allows the homilist to turn to that which led to exaltation: the suffering and death of Jesus. These verses recall the submission and exaltation of the Son in a way similar to Phil 2:6-11. With the use of the name "Jesus," the homilist calls to mind the concrete historical reality which was this man Jesus who "tasted death for everyone." It is Jesus who now becomes the subject of contemplation and source of encouragement for the community. The homilist's grounding in history and his looking toward the future are further made evident in the reference to the "world to come" in verse 5 and to the realistic statement that we do *not yet* see all things in subjection to the Son. For our homilist there is a future, a world to come, where that which was begun in Jesus will be brought to completion.

The second section (vss. 10-18) offers us the reason for the Son's suffering and what that means for humanity. As the portrayal of the Exalted Son of God was striking in its magnificence, so too that of Jesus—Brother of All Persons— is daring in the depth of unity it establishes between Jesus and his sisters and brothers. This section introduces the title for which Hebrews has traditionally been most famous: the faithful high priest. It also gives and defines the fruit of salvation in a characteristic way as sanctification (vs. 11) and expiation of sin (vs. 17).

Whereas the previous verses have eloquently stressed the supremacy of the name, person, and word of the Son of God over the angels and over all creation, 2:10-18 focuses on the unity of Jesus with all humankind and what that unity means. Weaving together several strands of thought, the homilist grounds the community in the security that they have a Savior who knows and understands their human existence and the suffering involved in their lives.

In order to stress Jesus' solidarity with humankind, the homilist tells us that the one who for whom and by whom all exists was himself made perfect (or brought to completion) by suffering. Further, Jesus and the community shared the same origin, and the same flesh and blood, the same nature. Jesus died as do all persons. He was made like us in all respects, and, like us, suffered and was tempted. Few texts in the New Testament stress so strongly the humanity of Jesus, few portray so graphically his profound immersion in our human existence.

N.B.

This unity in the existence and destiny of his sisters and brothers has produced a profound and existence-altering reality, according to the homilist. As a result of his sharing in our humanity, Jesus has become the pioneer of salvation and has sanctified those who follow him. Pioneer of their salvation is a unique title for Jesus and evokes the notion of one who leads others forward into a new land. Here we are told that Jesus leads brothers and sisters into glory— that is, as later texts make even more clear, into union with the Father. Jesus, as pioneer, has been "made perfect" through his passion and death. The idea that the Son of God has been made perfect is perhaps shocking to us. The Greek term used here is a complex one and is sometimes used as a technical term for a perfection which implies release from earthly, inferior reality and entrance into the perfect, heavenly realm. It is a term which our homilist likes and uses frequently. (See 5:9; 7:19, 28; 9:9; 10:1, 14; 11:40; 12:23.) We are given here a preliminary indication as to its meaning for him. It is closely connected with salvation and sanctification, and thus with communion with God. What is being said here is that Jesus, as Savior, was completed, brought to fulfillment in his death. Because of that death, all were sanctified and were made able to enter the salvation which is God's presence. All are now able to approach the seat of grace, as we are told in 4:16. It is important to note here that in this first reference to salvation, sanctification (removal of sin) stands as an equivalent description for what has been brought about.

The ramifications of this sanctification are further developed. Jesus is not ashamed to call us brother and sister. Using Old Testament quotes (2:12=Ps 22:22; 2:13=Is 8:17-

18), which are sprinkled through his language as certain idiomatic expressions are in ours, we are told that Jesus not only stands in solidarity with us, but that he is glad to! As brother sharing in our death he has freed all humankind from the basic fear which rules all of our lives. In his death Jesus has destroyed the very power of death (the devil, we are told) and enables us to fear death no longer. As it did not destroy our brother but completed him, so too it will not destroy us. The pioneer of our salvation has himself braved the path through death for us.

Jesus has become like humans, not angels, we are told. His concern is with the flesh and blood reality of humanity (with the children of Abraham) and not with the otherworldly angelic sphere. The reference to the seed of Abraham points, perhaps, to a Jewish community who would identify themselves as children of Abraham and, hence, as those saved by Jesus. Like his brothers and sisters in every way, Jesus has become the merciful and faithful high priest.

The high priest was an extremely important figure in the Judaic cult. Chosen from among the many priests, the high priest alone was permitted to enter into the inner sanctuary of the Temple (the Holy of Holies), to come directly into the presence of God. He did so on one particular feast, that of the Day of Atonement. On that day the high priest entered the sanctuary to offer expiation for his own sins and for the sins of his people.

Two ceremonies were involved in the ritual of the Day of Atonement. In the first, the high priest offered a bull as sacrifice for his own sin and for that of the priesthood as a whole. The high priest then entered the Holy of Holies to sprinkle the mercy-seat (considered to be the place of God's presence). The high priest next offered a goat for the sin of the people; this blood too was sprinkled on the mercy-seat. The second ceremony dealt with a second goat upon whose head all the sins of the people were symbolically placed. The goat which carried the sins of the people was taken into the desert and left there.

This feast, known to us as Yom Kippur, was the great day for the Israelites for on this day, in the action of the high priest, their guilt was removed and they were once again at peace with their God. The Day of Atonement is very important for the homilist and every element of its ritual will be commented upon in the following chapters.

The homilist assumes the community's knowledge of the significance of this feast and of the office of high priest. He establishes that Jesus has become the new high priest who, chosen from his people, enters the presence of God and offers sacrifice for sin, and removes from them the burden of their guilt.

Finally, we are told that Jesus not only knows what we experience but that he is able, as high priest, as pioneer of salvation, to help those who are tempted. The continuing merciful presence and intercession of this savior are placed before the eyes of the community once again.

II. JESUS: FAITHFUL AND MERCIFUL HIGH PRIEST. 3:1 – 5:10.

The second major section of the epistle begins with chapter 3. In this section the homilist develops the title which he gave to Jesus in 2:17: the merciful and faithful high priest. In a typical way, the development begins with the last adjective (faithful) and then in 4:15–5:10 the idea of Jesus as merciful high priest is treated.

JESUS AND MOSES.
3:1-6.

> **3** Therefore, holy brethren, who share in a heavenly call, consider Jesus, the apostle and high priest of our confession. ²He was faithful to him who appointed him, just as Moses also was faithful in God's house. ³Yet Jesus has been counted worthy of as much more glory than Moses as the builder of a house has more honor than the house. ⁴(For every house is built by some one, but the builder of all things is God.) ⁵Now Moses was faithful in all God's house as a servant, to testify to the things that were to be spoken later, ⁶but Christ was faithful over God's house as a son. And we are his house if we hold fast our confidence and pride in our hope.

Having portrayed the marvel of Jesus' solidarity with us, the homilist informs us that we are sharers in the destiny of Jesus. He then exhorts the community to look upon this Jesus the apostle and high priest of our belief. The term "apostle" here is not meant in a technical sense (as one of the twelve apostles) but in its more original sense of the emissary.

In 3:1-6 the fidelity of Jesus is compared to that of *the* great Old Testament figure Moses. Jesus is placed within the context of the history of Israel. Here the homilist comments on a well-known Old Testament text (Num 12:7) where we are told that God himself declares that he speaks directly to Moses for "he is entrusted with all my house" (12:7b). In rabbinic tradition Num 12:7 was taken as an indication that Moses was greater than the angels. Having established the Son's superiority over the angels, our homilist declares now that he is greater even than Moses. This superiority consists in the fact that, while Moses was a faithful servant over the people of Israel (the house built by God), Jesus was faithful as a *son* over the house.

The house built by God changes character and now the community itself becomes that house. The author places a condition on being the household, the new people of Israel: one must hold tightly to the confidence and hope we have been given. Once again the homilist stresses the necessity for our fidelity.

LISTEN TO HIS WORD *TODAY*.
3:7 – 4:14.

> [7]Therefore, as the Holy Spirit says,
> "Today, when you hear his voice,
> [8]do not harden your hearts as in the
>   rebellion,
> on the day of testing in the wilderness,
> [9]where your fathers put me to the
>   test
> and saw my works for forty years.

¹⁰Therefore I was provoked with that
     generation,
and said, 'They always go astray in
     their hearts;
they have not known my ways.'
¹¹As I swore in my wrath,
'They shall never enter my rest.' "

¹²Take care, brethren, lest there be in any of you an evil,
unbelieving heart, leading you to fall away from the living
God. ¹³But exhort one another every day, as long as it is
called "today," that none of you may be hardened by the
deceitfulness of sin. ¹⁴For we share in Christ, if only we
hold our first confidence firm to the end, ¹⁵while it is said,

"Today, when you hear his voice,
do not harden your hearts as in the rebellion."

¹⁶Who were they that heard and yet were rebellious? Was
it not all those who left Egypt under the leadership of
Moses? ¹⁷And with whom was he provoked forty years?
Was it not with those who sinned, whose bodies fell in the
wilderness? ¹⁸And to whom did he swear that they should
never enter his rest, but to those who were disobedient?
¹⁹So we see that they were unable to enter because of
unbelief.

4 Therefore, while the promise of entering his rest
remains, let us fear lest any of you be judged to have
failed to reach it. ²For good news came to us just as to
them; but the message which they heard did not benefit
them, because it did not meet with faith in the hearers.
³For we who have believed enter that rest, as he has said,

"As I swore in my wrath,
'They shall never enter my rest,' "

although his works were finished from the foundation
of the world. ⁴For he has somewhere spoken of the
seventh day in this way, "And God rested on the seventh
day from all his works." ⁵And again in this place he said,

"They shall never enter my rest."

⁶Since therefore it remains for some to enter it, and those
who formerly received the good news failed to enter

because of disobedience, [7]again he sets a certain day, "Today," saying through David so long afterward, in the words already quoted,

"Today, when you hear his voice,
do not harden your hearts."

[8]For if Joshua had given them rest, God would not speak later of another day. [9]So then, there remains a sabbath rest for the people of God; [10]for whoever enters God's rest also ceases from his labors as God did from his.

[11]Let us therefore strive to enter that rest, that no one fall by the same sort of disobedience. [12]For the word of God is living and active, sharper than any two-edged sword, piercing to the division of soul and spirit, of joints and marrow, and discerning the thoughts and intentions of the heart. [13]And before him no creature is hidden, but all are open and laid bare to the eyes of him with whom we have to do.

[14]Since then we have a great high priest who has passed through the heavens, Jesus, the Son of God, let us hold fast our confession.

Moving from the if-clause of 3:6 which pointed to the necessity of remaining firm in hope, the homilist now paints a rather menacing picture of what can happen to those who do not remain faithful. Using a long quote from Psalm 95 (vss. 7-11), the fate of the Israelites in the desert is given as lesson. Standing on the edge of entrance into the promised land, these people did not listen to God's word, they did not obey it. As a consequence, God became angry with them and they were not allowed to attain the end of their journey, to enter into God's rest. Rather, they were condemned to wander in the desert and never to enter the promised land.

Two important elements are introduced in this section. The first is that of apostasy. Hebrews 3:12, which warns against "an evil, unbelieving heart, leading you to fall away from the living God," uses the Greek word apostasy (the RSV uses "fall away"). Apostasy emerges as the great

danger to the Hebrew community. The example of the
Israelites evokes it here; in 6:4-8; 10:26-31; 12:16-17, 25 it
is addressed as a real and imminent danger. The second
element is that of judgment. Apostasy is seen as all the more
threatening because the final judgment of God is about to
take place. The community of the "Hebrews" are under a
double threat: their own rejection and the eschatological
judgment.

The homilist draws several lessons from this example.
In the first place, he tells us that *we* have heard a word
from God and had best heed it and believe in it, for we know
what happens to those who do not. Secondly, since the
Israelites did not enter God's rest (here 'rest' becomes a
place where one shares in the presence of God), the promise
of entrance still stands and is open to those who now hear
God's word. Thirdly, the homilist plays upon the word
"today" and declares that there is a new today, here and
now, when the word is addressed to God's people. *Therefore*,
let us be eager, he says, to enter into that rest. Let us not
be foolish and reject the word spoken to us today and in
turn lose our own entrance into God's presence, into the
promised land.

Once again we see the homilist's reliance on and freedom
with the Old Testament. He quotes, he plays upon significant
phrases (Today, they shall never enter my rest), he interprets, he combines (Ps 95 and the creation stories). It is this
freedom and familiarity with the Old Testament which
often make it hard for us to understand Hebrews. Unlike
the original community, we are not so easily at home with
Old Testament references or with the lessons they evoke.
Yet we *are* familiar with the temptation to give up, to dis-
regard the word of God addressed to us today and to take
lightly the gifts we have been given. We too are called to
account by God's word.

The seriousness of disobeying that word is stressed when
we hear the brief hymn to the word in 4:12-13. Here, in one
of the most well-known texts of Hebrews, we are told that
God's word reaches into our very depths and exposes all

that we are before God. This word, alive and active as it is, places us in a spotlight, as it were, naked before the one who speaks to us.

This section ends with a reminder that we have one who has entered into God's rest, who has gone through the heavens to the dwelling place of the Father. We have reason for confidence, we are told, so let us hold tight to our belief. Let us not lose what we have been given. This section, while difficult for us today because of its references to texts and events which seem obscure to us, reflects the basic tension of Hebrews *and* the basic message. We have been given so much, we have every reason for confidence, yet we stand in danger of losing that, of rejecting the gift. And woe to us if we do.

EXCURSUS I: THE HOMILIST AS EXEGETE— THE USE OF THE OLD TESTAMENT IN HEBREWS.

The homilist's frequent and diverse use of the Old Testament is obvious to us at this point as the complexity of Old Testament citations in 3:7 – 4:14 makes clear. It is perhaps a good idea to pause in our commentary for a few moments and to examine somewhat more carefully the many ways in which the Old Testament is used in Hebrews and the understanding of the Old Testament which is reflected in the homily.

If one sometimes has the feeling when reading Hebrews that one is confronted with a series of quotations and commentaries on these quotations, there is good reason for this. Although the exact number is sometimes disputed, Hebrews contains approximately 36 direct citations of the Old Testament and almost 80 instances where an Old Testament text is clearly referred to, even if not quoted exactly.

The majority of the citations and allusions comes from the Psalms and the Pentateuch. Many of the references are ones that were used in the Judaic liturgical cycle and would have been well-known to the original hearers of our homily. We know that the Old Testament existed in both the Hebrew (Masoretic) version and the Greek (Septuagint-LXX) version and at times these two versions differ as to the wording (and hence the meaning) of a text. Both versions are cited in the New Testament, but our homilist cites the Septuagint version exclusively. This fact is significant since it is an indication that the homilist came from a milieu which was Greek-speaking as opposed to a Hebrew-speaking, Judaic background. Further, the homilist's citations are remarkably exact and do not appear to be given from memory. It would seem, then, that he had a text before him to which he referred. This fact makes any change in an Old Testament citation a *significant* one and one made for a specific purpose.

The homilist uses the Old Testament in different ways. In some cases, he cites a single text and then applies it to the present situation. This is what happens in chapter 8 where Jeremiah 31:31-34 is cited. The homilist, in the longest Old Testament quotation in the New Testament, cites the full text of Jeremiah's promise of a new covenant in order to show that a new covenant was necessary *and* that it has come into being. This same principle is at work in Hebrews 12:26 where Haggai 2:6 is cited in order to point to a future event which the community must endure. What the Old Testament text does *not* say is also important to our homilist. In chapter 7, for example, the author makes use of Genesis 14:18-20 to establish the superiority of the priesthood of Melchizedek over the Levitical priesthood. He comments on Melchizedek's name, his title as King of Salem, and upon the fact that no mention is made of Melchizedek's parentage. This lack of reference in the Old Testament enables the homilist to assert that Melchizedek "continues a priest forever" (Heb 7:3).

At times, a certain Old Testament text is cited repeatedly and each time a different element of the text is stressed.

The homilist's use of Psalm 110 is an excellent example of this. In Hebrews 1:13, Psalm 110:1 ("Sit at my right hand, till I make thy enemies a stool for thy feet.") is cited in order to stress the exaltation of the Son of God. In Hebrews 5:6, 10, Psalm 110:4 with its reference to Melchizedek ("Thou art a priest forever, after the order of Melchizedek") becomes the introduction to a long discussion on the high priesthood of Jesus. In Hebrews 10:12, verse 1 of the Psalm is again cited in order to stress the triumph of the one who was sacrificed. The homilist has woven Psalm 110 into the very fabric of his homily, sometimes stressing one aspect, sometimes another. To a lesser extent, he applies the same principle to the new covenant text of Jeremiah 31. Cited in its entirety in Hebrews 8:8-12, the last section of this same prophecy is cited in Hebrews 10:16-17 in order to stress the forgiveness of sin realized in the new covenant.

In other cases, a whole series of citations are strung together in a chain-like fashion. Hebrews 1:5-13 is a good example of this process. In Hebrews 1:5-13 the homilist establishes the superiority of the Son in relation to the angels. He does so by calling upon the Scriptures themselves to speak. In these verses, where the Old Testament is cited seven times, the Old Testament texts stand alone. There is no commentary upon the texts, there are only phrases such as: "To which of the angels has he said. . ." (1:5, 13) which serve to link them together. Hebrews 1:5-14 presents a three-fold contrast between the Son and the angels: a) relationship as Son, relationship of subordination; b) the eternal position of the Son, the changeable position of the angels; c) the place of the Son at the right hand of God; the place of angels as sent to serve those who will inherit salvation. All of this is established by the Old Testament itself, says our homilist!

In yet other instances, the homilist combines two texts which appear to be unrelated but which contain an expression or phrase that allows them to be linked together. Hebrews 3:7 – 4:14 provides us with an example of this type of citation. Hebrews 3:7 – 4:14 begins with a citation of Psalm 95:7-8, inserts a citation of Genesis 2:2 (Heb 4:4), cites Psalm 95 twice more, and ends with a quotation of

Genesis 2:2 (Heb 4:10). Psalm 95 deals with an exhortation to heed the voice of God and recalls the wandering of the people of Israel in the desert; Genesis 2:2 recounts the last moment of creation when God rested. What connects these two texts for our homilist is the term "rest." The Israelites, unfaithful to God's word, were unable to enter into rest and were condemned to wander in the desert; God himself has entered into rest and God's rest still stands open to the Christians who hear and obey his word. The homilist first uses one text to establish the possibility of rest and the necessity of faith in order to attain that rest. In so doing he creates a sense of urgency in face of the possibility of its loss (cf. the repeated use of "today": 3:7, 13, 15; 4:7). He then uses another text (Gen 2:2) to clarify (for him, at least!) what he means by rest. The rest which the Israelites did not attain and the Christians must strive to reach is the very presence of God himself. To enter into rest is to enter into the presence of God who himself rests after the creation of the world. Entrance to God's presence is available to the believer and it is available now, says our homilist, and he uses two seemingly disparate texts to demonstrate this.

There are, finally, many many allusions to the Old Testament in Hebrews. The homilist appears to be someone so deeply steeped in Old Testament language that he uses it naturally, almost unconsciously. The description of the Sinai event in Hebrews 12:18-21 contains such allusions. In re-creating that event, the homilist alludes to the several Old Testament accounts (Ex 19:16-22; Dt 4:11-12; 5:22-27) and uses elements from each, in order to produce a scene which is both dramatic and terrifying.

The most extended series of allusions is found in chapter 11, however. Here, in order to call his community to a faith which perseveres, the homilist recounts the whole of the history of Israel. He does so from the perspective of the great men and women who served (and still serve!) as models of fidelity in the face of great difficulties. Person after person is presented for the encouragement of the weary "Hebrews," and significant moments in their lives, as recounted in the Old Testament, are recalled. Some, such as

Sarah, Abraham, and Moses, are well-known; others like Barak and Jephthah are unfamiliar to us. In each case, however, a phrase or a word echoes the Old Testament and calls upon the hearer to remember the whole story. This chapter is one of the most evocative in the New Testament and displays the homilist's great mastery of his Scriptures.

This same text provides us with an insight into one final characteristic of the homilist's use of the Old Testament: his freedom. Although citations from the Old Testament are very carefully made and remarkably accurate, the homilist is nonetheless very free in referring to Scriptures. That is, he does not hesitate to combine texts, to shorten them, or even to change them. Thus in Hebrews 12:21, the homilist presents us with a Moses who trembled in fear at Sinai while the Old Testament texts give no indication of any such terror on Moses' part. In Hebrews 12:26, Haggai 2:6 is cited, but by dropping sections of the original text, the homilist places special emphasis upon certain aspects of the Haggai prophecy.

The preceding examples of the various ways in which the Old Testament is used in Hebrews could be amplified by many more, but we have seen enough to recognize that the homilist knew the Old Testament *very* well and made many and varied uses of it in his preaching. We must now ask why he did so. What did the Old Testament mean to this person so convinced of the surpassing value of the new covenant? The first thing which is made evident is that the Old Testament is clearly the word of God for our homilist. No ordinary word, the Old Testament stands as divine revelation in which God speaks to his people. The introductions to the Old Testament citations make this clear. Except for one case (Heb 4:7 "saying in David"), there is no reference to the source of the texts; all come from God! Further, it is always God or his Spirit who speaks in the Scriptures. Our homilist never uses expressions like "the prophet says," or "it is written," or "the psalmist says." The Old Testament is God's word, one which God *speaks* to his people. All of the homilist's citations are faithful to the original insight of Hebrews 1:1: God has spoken.

For our homilist, the Old Testament is not a former word but one addressed now to the people. The citations are usually introduced by "he (God, Spirit) *says*," not "it was said." The revelation contained in Scripture is active and alive in Hebrews; it is a word which calls, invites and pierces to the very heart of the hearer (see Heb 4:12-13). The Old Testament is, finally, a word of promise which finds its fulfillment and takes on new meaning in light of the Christ-event. "God has spoken" in a Son (Heb 1:1-2). All that was promised and pointed to, be it forgiveness of sins, a new covenant, entrance into the promised land, all are realized now and made present in the Son who has saved us. The Christ-event illumines and fulfills the Old Testament and gives it an eschatological significance. The end-time has broken through in the Son, God has spoken fully, the last days are upon us.

The homilist's understanding of the Old Testament and his repeated citations of it give us, finally, an insight into the community called "Hebrews." Clearly they knew their Scripture! The homilist shows no need to introduce a text, to explain it, to cite a reference or to defend its revelatory character. He speaks to a community who share his reverence for God's word, who know the Scriptures and who can supply the unspoken background. This community, these "Hebrews" would have had no problem identifying (and identifying *with*) the great list of heroes and heroines named in chapter 11. They would have seen themselves as part of these people, as ones who joined God's people in the great chorus of praise made possible in Jesus.

This insight into the nature of the community gives rise to two reflections. In the first place, our own difficulty with Hebrews becomes more understandable. The Old Testament is not familiar to us, the hopes and promises it contains fail to move us as they did the "Hebrews." Secondly, some of the difficulties of our own preachers are perhaps explained: not only do we not know the Old Testament, many of us do not know the New Testament. Hence, we do not respond to God's word; it remains foreign to us, a strange, sometimes sterile body of literature. The homilist today cannot presume what the homilist of Hebrews could. Perhaps there is a challenge here to those of us who would preach the Good News.

JESUS, COMPASSIONATE HIGH PRIEST.
4:15 – 5:10.

15For we have not a high priest who is unable to sympathize with our weaknesses, but one who in every respect has been tempted as we are, yet without sin. 16Let us then with confidence draw near to the throne of grace, that we may receive mercy and find grace to help in time of need.

5 For every high priest chosen from among men is appointed to act on behalf of men in relation to God, to offer gifts and sacrifices for sins. 2He can deal gently with the ignorant and wayward, since he himself is beset with weakness. 3Because of this he is bound to offer sacrifice for his own sins as well as for those of the people. 4And one does not take the honor upon himself, but he is called by God, just as Aaron was.

5So also Christ did not exalt himself to be made a high priest, but was appointed by him who said to him,
"Thou art my Son,
today I have begotten thee";
6as he says also in another place,
"Thou art a priest for ever,
after the order of Melchizedek."
7In the days of his flesh, Jesus offered up prayers and supplications, with loud cries and tears, to him who was able to save him from death, and he was heard for his godly fear. 8Although he was a Son, he learned obedience

through what he suffered; [9]and being made perfect he became the source of eternal salvation to all who obey him, [10]being designated by God a high priest after the order of Melchizedek.

Our speaker turns now to the development of a second quality spoken of in 2:17: Jesus is a merciful high priest. He begins with a reminder of the solidarity of Jesus with his brothers and sisters followed by a brief exhortation (4:15-16). In the first ten verses of chapter 5, two qualifications of the priesthood are presented and we are shown how Christ eminently fulfills these qualifications.

The development of Jesus' whole sharing in human existence which was presented in chapter 2 is recalled here, but new thoughts are also introduced. Jesus is like us in all things, except sin, we are told. The speaker now makes explicit the sinlessness of Jesus in order to prepare for chapter 7 (especially vss. 26-27) where the sinlessness of the high priest becomes very important. Because we have such a one, we must, says our speaker, approach the throne of grace and we must do so boldly. The cultic tone of Hebrews, wherein the ritual sacrifice of the Old Testament is compared to the New Testament sacrifice in Jesus, is introduced in verse 16. We are told to *approach* the throne. The term used for "approach" is a cultic one used technically for one's approach to the divine in worship. It is a term which is used often in Hebrews (see also 7:25; 10:1, 22; 11:6; 12:18, 22) and which places the whole homily within a cultic framework.

We are to approach the throne of grace, that is, the presence of God and the place where one receives mercy. This throne recalls the "mercy seat" of Judaic cult. The mercy seat was actually at the top of the Ark of the Covenant. Considered as the seat of God, it was the place where God "met" Moses and spoke to him (Ex 25:22). The astonishing difference between the Old Testament mercy seat and the throne of grace in 4:16 lies in the fact that whereas only the high priest could approach the mercy seat, and did so with fear and trembling, all are told to approach the throne of grace, *and* to do so in confidence! Already suggested here, certainly to Judaic minds, is the vast difference which the sacrifice of Jesus has made in one's relationship to God.

The first four verses of chapter 5 establish two character- istics of the Judaic high priest. He is from among the people and hence is able to sympathize with them in their weakness in his offering of sacrifice for sins; he is, further, chosen by God. Since the time of Aaron, first high priest, it has been clear that God chooses the one who will fill this office. The individual does not.

Verses 5-10 are an application of these characteristics to Jesus. First we are told that God has appointed Christ (this title is used here for the first time). The Old Testament makes this clear. The one who has called Jesus "my son" (Ps 2:7, the first citation used in chapter 1:5) has made yet another declaration. "You are priest forever as was Mel- chizedek." Here the speaker cites Psalm 110 again (as he did in 1:13), but this time a later verse (vs. 4). He also drops the name Melchizedek into his homily.

Melchizedek is a mysterious figure who seems to have captured the imagination of the Israelites. In Genesis 14 Melchizedek was the King of Salem "priest of God most high" (Gen 14:18). He was host to Abraham after Abraham had won a great victory. Melchizedek brought out bread and wine and blessed Abraham. Abraham in turn gave a tenth of all that he possessed to Melchizedek. That is all we know of Melchizedek.

The combination of priesthood and kingship in the person of Melchizedek led to traditions which saw Melchizedek as the symbol of the great Messianic times when a Messiah who would be both priest and king would appear. Psalm 110, a hymn about the Messiah, draws upon such a tradition when it refers to Melchizedek. In Hebrews, the tradition is again employed. It is expanded upon in very elaborate and imaginative ways, particularly, as we shall see, in chapter 7.

Appointed by God, Jesus is nonetheless one of us. We are told that he prayed to God, that he cried out to God to be saved. There are no explicit references to actual events in the life of Jesus in Hebrews, but we have here perhaps a reference to the agony at Gethsemane where Jesus prayed for deliverance from what he was about to endure (see Mt 26:36-46; Mk 14:32-42; Lk 22:40-46). Whether the reference here is specifically to the Gethsemane accounts or to Jesus' passion in general is uncertain. One thing is certain, however; Jesus suffered the dregs of our human existence, he experienced what we all face and responded as all humans do—in anguish and in cries for help. Further, we are told that Jesus grew in his suffering, that he learned what it means to obey God's will. Jesus' cries were heard by God because of his awe and reverence (a better translation than "fear") for the one who could save him, and he was brought to perfection, fulfillment.

Because of this, he has become the source of unending salvation. Pioneer, apostle, source. In Jesus one touches a salvation which never ends, which never changes, which is always available to those who approach, who obey him. Merciful high priest, appointed by God, of the line of Melchizedek; so ends this elaboration of the statement in 2:17 "a merciful and faithful high priest." The speaker will eventually turn to a discussion of Jesus' priesthood, but first he addresses his community personally in yet another warning.

III. THE ONE, PERFECT SACRIFICE.
5:11 – 10:39

We come now to the heart of Hebrews. In these next chapters the meaning of Jesus' priesthood will be presented, and the significance of that priesthood for all Christians will be made to stand forth in all its wonder. The importance of this section is stressed in the very structure of the homily. The sections on high priesthood are introduced and concluded by long, severe exhortations. "Pay close attention to what I am saying/have just said for your lives depend on it," the community is told.

BEWARE OF FALLING AWAY!
5:11 – 6:12

[11]About this we have much to say which is hard to explain, since you have become dull of hearing. [12]For though by this time you ought to be teachers, you need some one to teach you again the first principles of God's word. You need milk, not solid food; [13]for every one who lives on milk is unskilled in the word of righteousness, for he is a child. [14]But solid food is for the mature, for those who have their faculties trained by practice to distinguish good from evil.

6 Therefore let us leave the elementary doctrines of Christ and go on to maturity, not laying again a foundation of repentance from dead works and of faith toward

29

God, ²with instruction about ablutions, the laying on of hands, the resurrection of the dead, and eternal judgment. ³And this we will do if God permits. ⁴For it is impossible to restore again to repentance those who have once been enlightened, who have tasted the heavenly gift, and have become partakers of the Holy Spirit, ⁵and have tasted the goodness of the word of God and the powers of the age to come, ⁶if they then commit apostasy, since they crucify the Son of God on their own account and hold him up to contempt. ⁷For land which has drunk the rain that often falls upon it, and brings forth vegetation useful to those for whose sake it is cultivated, receives a blessing from God. ⁸But if it bears thorns and thistles, it is worthless and near to being cursed; its end is to be burned.

⁹Though we speak thus, yet in your case, beloved, we feel sure of better things that belong to salvation. ¹⁰For God is not so unjust as to overlook your work and the love which you showed for his sake in serving the saints, as you still do. ¹¹And we desire each one of you to show the same earnestness in realizing the full assurance of hope until the end, ¹²so that you may not be sluggish, but imitators of those who through faith and patience inherit the promises.

Although the homilist has more to say of the high priesthood of Christ, he first changes the subject and turns abruptly to a direct admonition of the community. They are not able to hear what he has to say because they have become sluggish and no longer listen with eagerness. Perhaps we have here a subtle chiding of those individuals who are waiting for the homily to end, the first century equivalent to our present-day time-keepers and seat-squirmers!

The "Hebrews" are not ignorant of the message of faith and should be speaking that message themselves. Instead, they need to be taught again. They are like children who need to be spoon-fed. The homilist uses the comparison between baby food (milk) and that of an adult (solid food).

Paul uses the same image in 1 Cor 3:1-2 when he admonishes the Corinthian community for its immaturity.

In 6:1 our speaker apparently changes his mind for he says he will move on from the basic teachings (the ABC's) toward maturity. The Greek word translated as maturity is the same previously used to speak of the perfection/fulfillment of Jesus. Here it indicates a full growth in Christianity, a full understanding of what has happened in the event of the sacrifice of Jesus Christ. Some ABC's are mentioned as those teachings which must be left behind now. The basics spoken of in 6:1b-2 are very general and are not meant to be any kind of listing of fundamental doctrines. They are not even specifically christian teachings. The same elements are spoken of in the Judaic writings found at Qumran. They are merely some of the things the community should already know.

Having decided to move forward, the speaker uses the fact that the "Hebrews" are not infants in faith in order to give them a *very* frightening warning. The text of 6:4-8 is one of the most severe in the New Testament. The only verses which are even more harsh are those of Heb 10:26-31, which end this section. In both these texts the subject is the same as we have already encountered in 2:3 and 3:12: rejection of the gift of salvation.

Hebrews 6:4-6 (one sentence) are remarkable verses, both in content and in style. The sentence begins with what is really an exclamation: It is impossible! Then, however, a series of five participles are introduced before we are finally told (in vs. 6) what it is that is impossible. There are many contrasts in these verses: but the basic one is that of the goodness of the christian experience and the horror of the rejection of that experience. Several expressions are used to describe what it is to know salvation: One is enlightened, one tastes the heavenly gift, the good word of God and the powers of the coming age, one shares in the Spirit. Each of these phrases bespeaks a very real and profound experience wherein one recognizes and veritably savors the goodness of God in one's life. One also is given a foretaste, as it were, of the eschatological time, the coming age for which one hopes.

This whole glorious description is introduced by yet another theme-word: "once." "Once" is used throughout Hebrews to characterize those events which cannot be repeated, such as Jesus Christ's sacrifice. ("Once" is contrasted with the idea of repetition. In this case the repetition of Jesus' sacrifice.) For our homilist, those events which are not repeated are efficacious ones, the very notion of repetition indicates inadequacy. In 6:4-6 the initial time of conversion is described and characterized as a one-time, fully efficacious event. Portrayed so eloquently here is that time when, as adults, we take hold of grace and allow it to take hold of us. Such times *are* truly unrepeatable and, if we are faithful to them, they continue to give life to us. It is well to remember such times and to re-live their goodness.

But the "Hebrews" are not allowed to dwell in glowing memories. The series of descriptions ends abruptly with "and falling." The RSV has translated this as "if then they commit apostasy." This is true to the meaning of the text, but the dramatic abruptness of the original words is lost. There is no "if" in the original homily, there is rather a description of one who experiences the one-time, efficacious goodness of christian conversion and who falls away, who rejects that goodness.

For such a one, renewal to repentance is impossible. Another radical conversion cannot take place. This is a terrifying statement, and one which must be understood in terms of the author's stress upon the unique character of the christian event: it cannot be repeated, just as the crucifixion of Jesus is unrepeatable. For, says our homilist, to renew an apostate again to repentance implies crucifying the Son of God again (the RSV has only "crucify" but the literal sense is "crucify again") and holding him up for public shame for one's own benefit. Such a thought is not only reprehensible, it is unthinkable for our homilist. To repeat Jesus' sacrifice is to say the first one was, in fact, powerless.

A simple illustration from nature makes the either/or character of the matter eminently clear. The Christian is like the land which, receiving the rain of God's grace, either brings forth useful growth or bears useless weeds. For the former there is blessing, for the latter there is only curse and fire. There is no middle ground. There is only life or death. A stark message which reminds us once again of the approaching fiery eschatological judgment.

Happily, the homily does not end here, but goes on to assure us that where apostasy is a real and dangerous possibility, it has not yet taken place. The community of the "Hebrews" have not yet fallen away. Our homilist expresses confidence in them in fact. He calls them "beloved" and is sure of better things and of salvation among them. It is striking to notice the criteria he uses for his judgment of the community. They have worked; they have loved and served "the saints." That is, they serve each other. All Christians were called saints in the early community, all had been made holy by God. Once again we are reminded here that true Christianity mandates service of one another. Experience of grace compels ministry of service.

The homilist concludes this section by echoing his constant exhortation: hold fast to the hope you have been given. He goes a step further and urges them to imitate those who inherit the "promises." The mention of "promises" leads to a reflection on the promise of God in 6:13-20.

THE OATH OF GOD.
6:13-20.

> [13]For when God made a promise to Abraham, since he had no one greater by whom to swear, he swore by himself, [14]saying, "Surely I will bless you and multiply you." [15]And thus Abraham, having patiently endured, obtained

the promise. [16]Men indeed swear by a greater than themselves, and in all their disputes an oath is final for confirmation. [17]So when God desired to show more convincingly to the heirs of the promise the unchangeable character of his purpose, he interposed with an oath, [18]so that through two unchangeable things, in which it is impossible that God should prove false, we who have fled for refuge might have strong encouragement to seize the hope set before us. [19]We have this as a sure and steadfast anchor of the soul, a hope that enters into the inner shrine behind the curtain, [20]where Jesus has gone as a forerunner on our behalf, having become a high priest for ever after the order of Melchizedek.

In 6:12 the homilist has urged the community to imitate those who inherit the promises. Both the idea of inheritance and of promise (see chapter 4) are important in Hebrews. In chapter 11 we are presented with a whole history of Israel from the point of view of heroes/heroines of faith and their relationships to God's promises. Here the idea of promise is developed in two ways. The homilist recalls Abraham, the prime example of faith in the promise, and he stresses the surety of God's promise.

Abraham is the perfect example of one who waited upon God's promise. The text which is quoted here (Gen 22:16-17) repeats the oath God made to Abraham after Abraham had shown he was willing to sacrifice his only son. It should be recalled here that the promise made to Abraham was that he would have many descendants (as many as the stars in the sky). When Abraham prepared to sacrifice his only son, he was in fact showing his faith in God in an incredible way, for he was sacrificing what appeared to be the only realization of God's promise. God responded to such faith by sparing Isaac and thus ensuring a fulfillment of the promise.

Not only did God spare Isaac, he renewed his promise and did so with an oath. Here the argument becomes rather obscure to twentieth-century people for whom an oath is no longer an extremely serious thing. In a culture based upon the validity of one's word, however, an oath was a very serious and profound thing. The gospels point this out when Jesus warns against swearing oaths in the Sermon on the Mount (Mt 5:33-37).

One always swears an oath by someone or something greater than oneself. "Do you swear to tell the whole truth, so help you *God*. . .?" Our preacher reminds his people that since there is no one, no thing greater than God, God swore upon himself. His point here is that there was no need for an oath; God's word was enough. Yet because God wished to give undeniable assurance, he not only spoke his promise but also declared its surety by oath. There are, then, *two* absolutely unalterable things upon which to rest our hope: the promise and the oath of God.

The promise still holds, as we have heard in chapter 4, and so the Christian now has firm unalterable ground upon which to stand. The hope will not be disappointed, we are told, so seize it! The christian hope rests not merely upon God's oath to Abraham, but also upon Jesus who has attained salvation for us. Thus we have an anchor—a grounding-spot—for our souls. That is, our hope rests now in Jesus who has gone before us, who as fore-runner ("pioneer" 2:10) has entered the resting place of God.

The homilist uses an image from the old covenant cultic life here. When he speaks of a hope that enters "the inner shrine behind the curtain" (vs. 19), he is referring to the "tent of meeting" which was carried with Israel in the desert and to the fact that this tent was divided into two sections: the Holy Place (a room for worship) and the Holy of Holies. This last was set apart for God himself and the Ark of the Covenant rested there. There was a veil which separated the Holy of Holies from the rest of the tent, and only the high priest could enter into this inner sanctuary. Thus, when the homilist says that our hope enters into this shrine, he is indicating that all believers now have entrance into the dwelling place of God. There is no longer a division. Jesus has gone before us and has opened the way for all who "seize the hope."

JESUS: HIGH PRIEST ACCORDING TO THE ORDER OF MELCHIZEDEK.
7:1-10.

7 For this Melchizedek, king of Salem, priest of the Most High God, met Abraham returning from the slaughter of the kings and blessed him; ²and to him Abraham apportioned a tenth part of everything. He is first, by translation of his name, king of righteousness, and then he is also king of Salem, that is, king of peace. ³He is without father or mother or genealogy, and has neither beginning of days nor end of life, but resembling the Son of God he continues a priest for ever.

⁴See how great he is! Abraham the patriarch gave him a tithe of the spoils. ⁵And those descendants of Levi who receive the priestly office have a commandment in the law to take tithes from the people, that is, from their brethren, though these also are descended from Abraham. ⁶But this man who has not their genealogy received tithes from Abraham and blessed him who had the promises. ⁷It is beyond dispute that the inferior is blessed by the superior. ⁸Here tithes are received by mortal men; there, by one of whom it is testified that he lives. ⁹One might even say that Levi himself, who receives tithes, paid tithes through Abraham, ¹⁰for he was still in the loins of his ancestor when Melchizedek met him.

Picking up on the last word of chapter 6, the homilist dwells now upon Melchizedek and provides us with a remarkable commentary on the brief mention of him in Genesis 14:18-20. In this text it is said that Melchizedek, "priest of God Most High," brought out bread and wine and blessed Abraham who was returning from his successful rescue of his kinsman Lot. In 7:1-2, he recalls the text and quotes the titles "king of Salem, priest of the Most High God." The commentary which follows is an excellent example of Judaic midrash, a method of taking apart the text and assigning meaning to almost every word. This method also finds meaning in what the text does not say.

Our homilist takes the name Melchizedek and translates it. Melchizedek can come from the Hebrew *malak* which means king, and *zedek* which means righteousness in Hebrew. Further, Salem comes from the Hebrew *shalom*— peace. Next, the homilist interprets what is *not* said. Since Genesis makes no reference to Melchizedek's origin or to his death, we are to conclude that he is eternal and thus is priest for eternity.

In verses 4-10 the reference to the tithes which Abraham gave and the blessing he received are commented upon. Here the commentary reaches its most elaborate point. As Abraham gave offerings to Melchizedek, so too the descendants of Abraham gave tithes to the current priesthood, the Levitical priesthood. But Melchizedek blessed Abraham and since the superior blesses the inferior, Melchizedek was superior to Abraham. Further, it could even be said that Melchizedek received tithes from Levi (the first of the Levitical priests) because Levi, as descended from Abraham, was "in the loins" of Abraham when he paid the tithes. To us it is amazing what our homilist could find in a few verses of the Old Testament. To his original hearers who were used to this method of argument, his commentary would have been more easily understood and the commentator admired for his agility.

Since the implicit argument as to the inferiority of the Levitical priesthood in verses 4-10 becomes explicit in verses 11-28, it is well for us to stop for a moment and recall the development of the Levitical order of priests. During Israel's formation in the desert, we are told that God set apart the tribe of Levi to carry the Ark of the Covenant which contained the tablets of the covenant, and to "stand before the Lord to minister to him" (Deut 10:8). The members of this tribe became the priests of Israel who were set apart for service of the sacred. There were no special personal qualifications for priesthood, it was not a vocation but rather an hereditary office. One needed only to be a descendant of Levi. The priest functioned in service of a sanctuary (a holy place). Eventually all priesthood centered around the Jerusalem temple where the priests offered sacrifice for the people. The priest, and especially the high priest, became the minister of the altar and placed upon the altar the sacrifices which he offered for the people and for himself. We hear of high priests in the Gospels, the chief of the priests who served the Jerusalem temple. While most of the references are unfavorable in the Gospels, it is important to remember that the office itself was *very* important to the people. The high priest stood as the ultimate mediator who offered prayer and sacrifice on behalf of the people and who obtained mercy and forgiveness from God for these same people.

When Hebrews speaks of the Levitical priesthood, it speaks of an institution deeply rooted in Israelite tradition; and when it criticizes this priesthood, it criticizes an integral part of Judaic life and a revered tradition. Our homilist not only criticizes it, he says it no longer has meaning. Further, the homilist connects the Levitical priesthood with the Judaic Law and criticizes the Law. Here it is necessary to understand that for the people of Israel the Law was not merely a system of precepts and regulations but rather the very charter of their existence as God's people. Keeping the Law meant keeping fidelity to the God who had chosen them and had made them his people in covenant. In what seem to us to be obscure statements our homilist is really making radical and potentially offensive claims.

JESUS: PRIEST OF THE ORDER
OF MELCHIZEDEK.
7:11-28.

> [11]Now if perfection had been attainable through the Levitical priesthood (for under it the people received the law), what further need would there have been for another priest to arise after the order of Melchizedek, rather than one named after the order of Aaron? [12]For when there is a change in the priesthood, there is necessarily a change in the law as well. [13]For the one of whom these things are spoken belonged to another tribe, from which

no one has ever served at the altar. ¹⁴For it is evident
that our Lord was descended from Judah, and in con-
nection with that tribe Moses said nothing about priests.

¹⁵This becomes even more evident when another priest
arises in the likeness of Melchizedek, ¹⁶who has become
a priest, not according to a legal requirement concerning
bodily descent but by the power of an indestructible life.
¹⁷For it is witnessed of him,
> "Thou art a priest for ever,
> after the order of Melchizedek."

¹⁸On the one hand, a former commandment is set aside
because of its weakness and uselessness ¹⁹(for the law
made nothing perfect); on the other hand, a better hope
is introduced, through which we draw near to God.

²⁰And it was not without an oath. ²¹Those who formerly
became priests took their office without an oath, but this
one was addressed with an oath,
> "The Lord has sworn
> and will not change his mind,
> 'Thou art a priest for ever.' "

²²This makes Jesus the surety of a better covenant.

²³The former priests were many in number, because
they were prevented by death from continuing in office;
²⁴but he holds his priesthood permanently, because he
continues for ever. ²⁵Consequently he is able for all time
to save those who draw near to God through him, since he
always lives to make intercession for them.

²⁶For it was fitting that we should have such a high
priest, holy, blameless, unstained, separated from sinners,
exalted above the heavens. ²⁷He has no need, like those
high priests, to offer sacrifices daily, first for his own
sins and then for those of the people; he did this once for
all when he offered up himself. ²⁸Indeed, the law appoints
men in their weakness as high priests, but the word of the
oath, which came later than the law, appoints a Son who
has been made perfect for ever.

The fact that another has come forth who is priest of the
superior order of Melchizedek is indication to our homilist

that the Levitical priesthood was unable to do what it was intended to do. It was incapable of attaining perfection. Here we have a contrast with previous statements which said that Jesus, in his sacrifice, was made perfect and became pioneer (2:10) and cause of salvation (5:9). Jesus is not of the Levitical tribe, that is of the order of Aaron (Aaron, brother of Moses, was traditionally seen as the first of Israel's priests). He is, rather, of the tribe of Judah. Once again the homilist argues from what the text does not say: since Moses said nothing about priesthood in regard to the tribe of Judah, there were no priests in this tribe.

Since the priesthood mediates the law to the people, when the priesthood changes, the law too is changed. The change in law is made clear when one recognizes that Jesus was not made priest according to this law but rather by the power of God. Once again Psalm 110:4 is quoted to substantiate Jesus' priesthood according to God's decree. The homilist then says that the former law has been set aside because it was weak and useless. In contrast to Jesus, it could bring nothing to fulfillment. The homilist has just dismissed the very foundations of Judaic life. If his hearers were of Judaic background and were tempted to return there, these statements would anger them, perhaps, and make them uncomfortable, certainly. Our time of rapid and radical changes, our sometimes apparent discarding of traditions take on new perspective in light of Hebrews. The homilist was convinced of one thing: the power of Jesus' sacrifice to sanctify once and for all. Anything and everything which interfered with faith in that was to be rejected. The law, then, is done away with and is replaced—not by a new law— but by a new and qualitatively different *hope*, a hope which allows us to approach God.

A further comparison with Levitical priesthood in verses 20-22 recalls what was said about God's unchangeable oath in 6:13-18, and—once again—cites Psalm 110:4. Here the homilist refers to the first phrase of Psalm 110:4: "The Lord swore" and establishes the fact that Jesus was made priest by God's unalterable oath whereas Levitical priests were not so established. Law and priesthood were essential com-

ponents of the relationship between Israel and her God—a
relationship known as a covenant. In the homilist's viewpoint a change in law and priesthood implies a change in
the covenant. In 7:22, then, the idea of a *new* covenant is
introduced when we are told that Jesus, by God's oath, also
becomes the guarantee of a better (completely other)
covenant.

The importance of Jesus' eternal priesthood becomes
clear when the homilist compares Jesus to the Levitical
priests. Since these priests died, they were of necessity
replaced by others, hence there were *many* Levitical priests.
Not so Jesus: priest forever, he is unique and needs no
replacement. Further he lives *always* to make intercession,
to mediate between God and his people. Jesus, always alive,
always mediator, saves completely those who come to God
through him.

This is the kind of high priest we needed, says our
homilist, not many priests who had to continuously offer
sacrifice both for their sins and the sins of the people. We
needed *one* who would offer sacrifice *once* for all, one who
was himself sinless and therefore needed only to offer for
the sins of others. We do have such a one: Jesus who has
made the one sacrifice, the perfect offering—himself.

The chapter ends with a final comparison: the law appoints men who, because of their own weaknesses, cannot
offer a perfect sacrifice. God's oath came after the law and
thus indicated the law was imperfect. This oath appoints
the Son, the One who has been made perfect forever. (See,
once again, 2:10 and 6:13-18.)

JESUS, MINISTER OF A NEW AND
BETTER COVENANT.
8:1-13.

8 Now the point in what we are saying is this: we have
such a high priest, one who is seated at the right hand of
the throne of the Majesty in heaven, ²a minister in the
sanctuary and the true tent which is set up not by man

but by the Lord. ³For every high priest is appointed to offer gifts and sacrifices; hence it is necessary for this priest also to have something to offer. ⁴Now if he were on earth, he would not be a priest at all, since there are priests who offer gifts according to the law. ⁵They serve a copy and shadow of the heavenly sanctuary; for when Moses was about to erect the tent, he was instructed by God, saying, "See that you make everything according to the pattern which was shown you on the mountain." ⁶But as it is, Christ has obtained a ministry which is as much more excellent than the old as the covenant he mediates is better, since it is enacted on better promises. ⁷For if that first covenant had been faultless, there would have been no occasion for a second.

⁸For he finds fault with them when he says:
"The days will come, says the Lord,
when I will establish a new covenant with the
    house of Israel
and with the house of Judah;
⁹not like the covenant that I made with their fathers
on the day when I took them by the hand
to lead them out of the land of Egypt;
for they did not continue in my covenant,
and so I paid no heed to them, says the Lord.
¹⁰This is the covenant that I will make with the
    house of Israel
after those days, says the Lord:
I will put my laws into their minds,
and write them on their hearts,
and I will be their God,
and they shall be my people.
¹¹And they shall not teach every one his fellow
or every one his brother, saying, 'Know the Lord,'
for all shall know me,
from the least of them to the greatest.
¹²For I will be merciful toward their iniquities,
and I will remember their sins no more."

[13]In speaking of a new covenant he treats the first as obsolete. And what is becoming obsolete and growing old is ready to vanish away.

One is tempted to imagine a drum roll here, or at least a raised voice as the author makes his main point: we have this perfect high priest which I have so eloquently described. Having established the vast superiority of Jesus' priesthood over that of the Levitical order, the homilist reminds the community once again of what it is they possess in faith: a perfect priest, seated at the right hand of God, living to intercede and save those who come to him (see 7:25).

Having made this point, the homilist makes another comparison between Jesus' priesthood and the Levitical one. He compares the cultic ministry of each in terms of the sacredness of the place wherein they serve and the sacrifices they offer. The comparison is difficult for us to understand without some background information. In the first place, priesthood implied the offering of sacrifices for the people of Israel. Now, if Jesus were on earth, he could not offer sacrifice since there are others who offer the sacrifices as prescribed by the law. Implied here is all the homilist has said about Jesus' sacrifice of himself, once for all (7:27). There is also a possible indication of the date of Hebrews here. If the reference to the priests who offer sacrifice is to be taken literally, the homily would have been delivered before 70 A.D., for we know that cultic sacrifice ended with the destruction of the Jerusalem temple.

Further, every Old Testament priest served a sanctuary, a holy place. The more sacred the sanctuary was considered to be, the more important was the priesthood. This idea gradually led to a concentration of the priesthood around *the* sacred place: the Jerusalem Temple. Here the homilist compares the sacredness of the throne of God with another tabernacle. This was the tent constructed by the Israelites in the desert in order to house the Ark of the Covenant in

which the tablets, written by the finger of God, were pre-
served. The tent traveled with the people and was considered
the place where God came to be with his people. It was here
that Moses met and spoke with God, that he learned of
God's will, and that he interceded for his people.

According to the Old Testament this first tent was built
according to very specific instructions which Moses received from God. Not only did Moses receive instructions,
he was also shown a model of what the sanctuary was to
look like. Moses then built the Ark and the tent according
to God's instructions and according to the model he was
shown. The homilist cites the instruction to Moses (Ex
25:40) in verse 5. While these instructions as they are
recounted in the Book of Exodus are seen as indications
of the sacredness and greatness of the Ark and the tent and
the Levitical priesthood, our homilist gives them a negative
interpretation. They were not the *real* things, he says, only
copies. By implication, then, the old covenant sanctuary
and the priesthood which served it were inferior in comparison to the priesthood of Jesus and the sanctuary which
he serves. If we keep in mind that the first tent was considered to be so holy because the tablets of the covenant
were housed in it, the turn of thought to the new covenant is
not such an obscure one.

As the Levitical priests were cultic ministers in the old
covenant sanctuaries, Jesus is minister (the Greek word
used for "minister" is a liturgical one) in the heavenly
sanctuary. As they ministered according to the old covenant,
Jesus mediates the new covenant. Jesus' ministry is a more
excellent one to the same degree that the new covenant is
more excellent than the old covenant. The new covenant and
Jesus' relationship to it were already mentioned in 7:20-22,
but now they become the focus of the homilist's attention.
New covenant is treated here, in chapter 9, in chapter 10,
and in chapter 13. In addition, the long and dramatic comparison of 12:18-24 is really a comparison of the two
covenants. So important is this idea, Hebrews has been
called the "Epistle of the New Covenant." New covenant

for our homilist means above all new relationship between God and the people, a new relationship made possible by the forgiveness of sin.

Here in 8:6-7, three important points are made about the new covenant: Jesus is the mediator of this covenant; it is a covenant based on better promises; it was necessary that a new covenant be established.

All priesthood was seen as mediation. The priest is the one who goes before God on behalf of the people, who brings their needs, their guilt before the Almighty, who seeks God's blessing and forgiveness, often by means of offering sacrifice for sins. The priest is also the one who obtains that forgiveness and blessing, who speaks God's word to the people. The mediator is the person who stands between God and his people, who also stands *for* both. In the mediator divine and human approach each other. While there were many who functioned as mediators when the old covenant was in force, Jesus alone is mediator of a new covenant. He alone is perfect mediator who, fully one with his people, encounters God in his dwelling place and attains full forgiveness of sin. His sacrifice is the perfect one which brings about the new order described in 8:8b-13.

This new covenant is established on better promises since it is established upon the oath of God. It is important here to recall 6:13-18, concerning the unchangeability of God's oath, and 7:20-22 where Jesus' constitution by oath as priest is presented. The new covenant is grounded upon these promises of God. Nothing, therefore, can prevent its accomplishment. The idea of promise is an important one for our homilist and one he repeats several times. The promises of God connote the two elements so vitally important for the community: first, they stand in the future as not yet fully completed. One has the promise of rest in chapter 4, for example, but one has not yet fully attained that sharing in God's rest. Secondly, the very fact of the promises is guarantee that they will be realized. We have—already—the promises themselves; and, in this case, since *God* is the one who has made them, they are absolutely certain of accomplishment. God's promise can never be doubted. The new covenant is grounded upon *better* promises because it is grounded upon better sacrifice and better mediation, that of Jesus made high priest by oath.

This new covenant was necessary, says our homilist, because the first was faulty and weak. The very fact of the promise of a second points to the imperfection of the first. We must remember here that repetition implies imperfection in Hebrews, and that a later reality is always greater than a former one. Thus, a second and later covenant shows clearly that the first was ineffectual.

Our homilist turns once again to the Old Testament for proof. The existence of the promise of a new covenant in the Book of Jeremiah shows that the first covenant established at Sinai was imperfect. The homilist says that God himself spoke these words and, in so doing, found fault with the first covenant while at the same time ordaining another, perfect one.

What follows in verses 8-12 is the longest citation of the Old Testament in the New. It is more than that, however. Jeremiah 31:31-34 remained one of the great hopes of God's people. Spoken to the Israelites in the midst of persecution and exile, it was promise of new, restored relationship between God and his people. Made at a moment when it seemed that God had abandoned his people, Jeremiah's prophecy was promise that, despite all evidence to the contrary, God was indeed faithful and would bring his people to a new and a better union with him.

Two elements of this prophecy are especially important to our homilist. First, each person shall come to knowledge of God, there will be no need for special teachers or intermediaries or for external laws. Rather, knowledge of and relationship to God would be an interior reality "written on the heart" of every person. Second, God will forgive the sins of his people. As we shall see, this forgiveness is the focal point for our homilist. It is *the* reality attained once and for all by the sacrifice of Jesus.

Verse 13 is a commentary on the Jeremiah text which develops the significance of the word 'new.' If there is need for a 'new' then the 'old' is obsolete and, we are told, ready to disappear. What we have here is a saying which resembles our twentieth century consumerism. This year's model makes last year's outmoded. There are three important differences, however. In the first place, "last year's" didn't work; the car didn't run. The covenant could not effect what it was supposed to effect. Secondly, *God* has established the new covenant and thereby brought about the hoped-for reality never before achieved. Finally, the second covenant is the perfect covenant and hence the last one. There will be no third covenant.

EXCURSUS II: JESUS CHRIST MEDIATOR— THE CHRISTOLOGY OF HEBREWS

With the statement that Jesus is mediator of a better covenant in Hebrews 8:6, the homilist has added yet another element to an already rich and complex presentation of his understanding of the significance of the Christ-event. Hebrews has been called an extended midrash (commentary) on Psalm 110, an Epistle of Priesthood, and the Epistle of the New Covenant. While all of these titles recognize significant aspects of the homily, Hebrews is first and foremost a Christological document. From the first sentence where we are told that God has spoken to us in a Son (1:2), to the final doxology "May the God of peace. . . through Jesus Christ to whom be glory for ever, amen" (13:20-21), the homilist bases all that he has to say upon the fact of Jesus Christ and upon the salvation brought into being in Jesus, Son of God.

The scope of the Christology of Hebrews is truly enormous and provides one with yet another insight into the giftedness of the unknown homilist. A listing of the numerous Christological titles in Hebrews makes this evident: Jesus is called Son (1:2; 3:6; 4:14; 5:8; 7:28), heir (1:2), radiance of the glory of God (1:3), author of salvation (2:10), high priest (2:17; 3:1; 4:14; 5:5; 5:10; 7:26; 8:1), apostle (3:1), forerunner (6:20), guarantee of a better covenant (7:22), mediator of the new (better) covenant (8:6; 9:15; 12:24), author and perfecter of our faith (12:2), our Lord Jesus (13:20), the great shepherd of the sheep (13:20). Beyond the many titles, Jesus Christ is presented as the pre-existent Son who became *truly* human, who suffered an ignominious death and thereby attained forgiveness of sin, who was raised from the dead to take his seat at the right hand of God where he now makes intercession for his people. All of the images, from the elaborate descriptions of priesthood and sacrifice to the hope-filled presentation of the new covenant, serve to enflesh the meaning of the Christ-event and to bring home most forcefully the significance of Jesus in the life of the Christian. Because the Christological reality is so very basic to Hebrews, and because it is frequently expressed in images foreign to twentieth century Christians, we will pause for a few moments here to clarify and synthesize what it is that Hebrews has to tell us about Jesus the Christ.

The Christology of Hebrews is primarily about relationships. We are never told that Jesus existed in Nazareth, that he preached or cured the sick; such knowledge is presumed. Rather, we are told what this man Jesus means, who he is in relationship to God, to the old covenant, to/for the believer. It is from this aspect of relationship that we will examine the Christology of Hebrews, beginning briefly with the Son's relationship to the angels, then looking at Jesus' standing in relation to the old covenant, to God, and to us. Finally, we will look again at Jesus as mediator, a phrase which perhaps best sums up the homilist's thought.

Jesus is seen in relationship to the angels in both chapters 1 and 2. In chapter 1, his superiority to the angels is firmly established (1:4-14). Jesus is Son, the angels are ministering servants. Jesus is seated at the right hand of the throne of majesty, the angels are sent here and there to serve those who will inherit salvation. In chapter 2, however, Jesus is shown as one made lower than the angels. Having portrayed the magnificence of the Son who is unquestionably greater and wholly other than the angels, the homilist offers a glimpse of the enormity of the act of salvation. This exalted one was made lower than the angels (2:9) in order that he might know death, and that he might know it on behalf of every person. In relating Jesus to the angels, God's superior beings, the homilist establishes a pattern which continues throughout Hebrews: the glorious Son who for the sake of humankind becomes the abased and suffering brother.

If we turn to the old covenant, out of which comes the majority of the images in Hebrews, we see that Jesus stands in a relationship of belonging to the old covenant, fulfilling it, surpassing it and even ending it. Jesus belongs to the old covenant, he is a true son of Israel. The "Hebrews" are reminded that he took on the seed of Abraham, not the nature of angels (2:16), and that he came from the tribe of Judah, not that of Levi (7:13-14). Member of the people of God, Jesus stands in comparison to that other great son of Israel: Moses. Moses, faithful to God (3:2, 5), is nonetheless inferior to Jesus, for while Moses was faithful as servant, Jesus was so as Son. The greatest figure of old covenant history is thus dwarfed next to Jesus, Son over the household of God (3:6).

More than individuals, however, it is the institutions of the old covenant which are fulfilled and surpassed in Jesus. In the first place, Jesus brings to completion the old covenant itself. Viewed by our homilist as imperfect, inefficacious, and ready to vanish, the old covenant is indeed done away with and the new is inaugurated—in Jesus. He is the guarantee (7:22) and mediator (8:6; 9:15; 12:24) of the new dispensation, the new age in which sin is finally forgiven and it is at last possible for the believers to approach their God.

In the second place, Jesus surpasses and ends the old covenant institution of the Levitical priesthood. Jesus as priest performs the actions of the old covenant cultic priesthood: he offers sacrifice for sins (7:27); he is mediator between God and the people (8:6); he enters into the holy place to attain purification (9:12). In each of these acts, however, he is superior to the Levitical priests: his sacrifice is his very self; his mediation is totally efficacious; he enters into the *true* holy place—the very presence of God; it is his own blood which purifies. Like the Levitical priests, Jesus shares in the humanity of his people and, as one of them, understands their weakness and the temptations they endure. It is, therefore, with compassion that he offers sacrifice for sins. Unlike the Levitical priests, Jesus has no need to offer sacrifice for his *own* sins; his ministry is solely for the sake of others.

While Jesus is shown to have shared in and fulfilled many basic characteristics of the old covenant cultic priesthood, it is the uniqueness of Jesus which interests the homilist. Jesus is someone completely other than those who have gone before him, and it is this fact which our homilist stresses when he develops the image of Jesus as high priest. In the first place, Jesus is not portrayed as priest of the Levitical order but of that order which precedes the priesthood of Aaron and which endures forever. Jesus is priest of the order of Melchizedek (6:20), an order vastly superior to any other, according to our homilist. Secondly, Jesus was appointed priest by an unalterable oath of God (7:28). There can be no doubt about the validity of his office! Further, Jesus is unique in that he offered only one sacrifice. Whereas all other priests repeatedly make sacrifice for sins, Jesus did so only once and by his one sacrifice put an end to all others. The final and most important characteristic of Jesus' unique priesthood grounds all the others: Jesus' single sacrifice was a perfect one which achieved what no other offering had been able to do. It attained true and lasting forgiveness of sin (9:12). Jesus is unique in that he has done what no one else has ever done, and our homilist forcefully portrays the unparalleled efficacy of Jesus' act by means of an extended, multifaceted comparison between his ministry and one of the most sacred of the old covenant institutions: its priesthood. Son of Israel, Jesus stands in special relationship to all of the old covenant as the one who brings it to completion and, in the eyes of our homilist, to an end.

Son of Israel, Jesus is also first-born Son of God. The homilist is concerned to establish a profound and vibrant relationship between Jesus and the Father. In this relationship it is above all as *Son* that Jesus is presented. From the very first sentence, Jesus is portrayed as first-born, well-beloved Son of God; and, as Son, he is obedient to the Father and faithful to him. Further, this Son is now re-united to God and seated at the right hand of God, he makes intercession for us.

God's relationship to Jesus is a dynamic one, it is God who acts and who is the ultimate source of the Son's activity. God speaks in his Son, appoints him heir of all things, creates the very world through him (1:1-3). It is, further, God who appoints Jesus High Priest (5:10), who perfects Jesus (5:9) and brings him to fulfillment (7:28), who hears his cry of anguish (5:7) and who raises him from the dead (13:20). The homilist views this relationship as being so close and so profound that he declares dramatically that Jesus is the very radiance of the glory of God and the representation of God's reality (1:3). One author has said that to see Christ is to see what the Father is like (F.F. Bruce, *The Epistle to the Hebrews*, p.6). To this we might well add: to see the Son acting is to recognize the Father's movement.

We must ask, finally, how this exalted and glorious Son stands in relationship to the people. Is Jesus Christ Son of God so glorious and exalted that he remains removed from the community known as the "Hebrews"? To the contrary, Jesus is equally close to the believer and equally involved in his/her life. Jesus is, quite simply, like us. Like us in all things save sin, Jesus is one with humankind. Unashamed, he calls us brothers and sisters (2:11). Because he is truly one with us, he understands us and knows what it is to walk the earth as free and yet not free; he knows the temptations we face, our tendency to discouragement, our fear and lack of courage. He understands our suffering, we are told, and he is, therefore, merciful to us and able to help us. As Jesus is truly Son of God, so too he is truly human, he is the one who knows, who understands, who cares.

Jesus Christ is not only *like* us, he is also *for* us. He is on our side and it is for our sake that he has acted and continues to act. He has suffered death for everyone (2:9), he offered his own self for our sins (7:27), he bore the sins of many (9:28) that he might attain eternal redemption for us (9:12). Jesus has opened a new and living way for us (10:19-20), he has enabled those who are called to receive the promise of an eternal inheritance (9:15) because he has, in his self-offering, purged our consciences from dead works that we might serve the living God (9:14). By means of Jesus' sacrifice for us, we are sanctified (10:10; 13:12) and brought to perfection (10:14). Finally, Jesus continues to act for us. He appears in the presence of God in our behalf (9:24) and there he intercedes for us (7:25).

The relationship between the believer and the Son of God is one so deep it penetrates the very marrow of one's existence. Because, and only because, Jesus is like and for his sisters and brothers, they are given a new identity. They are something new, who have a new thing, and who are called to a new existence. The believers are now partakers of Christ (3:14), members of his household, they share in his life and his destiny as fully as he shared in theirs (2:14). Freed from fear of death (2:15), saved and enabled to serve (9:14), the believers are new people who enter the presence of God with boldness (10:19-20). They are something new because of what they now have: the perfect high priest (8:1) who is able to save those who come to God through him (7:25). Having this high priest, believers are called to obey him (5:9) and to follow him. The homilist evokes a picture of this one who is so like them, who is so powerful on their behalf, who frees the "Hebrews" and enables them to come to God. He urges his community to look to Jesus, the beginning and end of our faith (12:2), to contemplate this one who endured so much (12:3). The believers are to join with him in praise of

God (12:22-24), they are to go unto him and to share in his shame (13:13). Ultimately, Jesus is model for the "Hebrews;" he is the one who in his life and death shows the believer what it is to be an obedient and faithful child of God. Living now, interceding now, Jesus Christ makes possible that to which he calls the believers. Forerunner (6:20), he enables them to follow him, to be with him in God's presence.

A review of the ways the homilist views Jesus Christ in relation to angels, the old covenant, to God, and to human-kind confirms one's original impression that the Christology of Hebrews is complex and all-pervasive. It also shows us how vast is the image of Jesus Christ in Hebrews, how this image reaches to highest exaltation in the glorified Son of God at the same time that it presents us with a complete, irreversible bonding between Jesus Christ and humankind. The homilist's view of Jesus takes many forms and multiple expressions, as we have seen, but perhaps the most felicitous one is that of mediator, for all that Jesus Christ is and does can be seen to come under the rubric of mediation. Briefly, mediation is a process of bringing together two opposing parties or forces. The mediator is the one who effects this conciliation.

According to our homilist's viewpoint, all of the history of God's people represents failed attempts at mediation. The mighty, living God remains on one side, the people on the other. The two remain continuously separated by the chasm of sin. Humankind has been unable to bridge that chasm, no matter how it tried. The Exodus was not truly successful for it did not bring the people to share the rest of God. The old covenant could not bring about removal of sin; it was imperfect and ripe for disappearance. The cult with its ritualized seeking of forgiveness was ineffectual. Even the great celebration of atonement only achieved external purity; the sacrifices didn't work, the priests were incapable of performing their most important ministry: attaining the forgiveness of sin for themselves and their people. There was no true encounter with God in the old covenant, not even at

Sinai. There were only fear, delusion, and, on the part of the great heroes and heroines of the old covenant, dogged hope and persistent, unsuccessful striving.

Only Jesus is true mediator. Only he brings about reconciliation. The two sides are not merely brought together by Jesus, they are united in him. The very radiance of God is—at the same time—like us in all things. The chasm is filled in Jesus, Son of God, brother of humankind. The care which the homilist takes to convince his listeners that Jesus is truly one with God and also truly one with humanity takes on a new significance here. Jesus must be fully both if reconciliation is to take place. Jesus Christ, perfect mediator, effects the perfect mediation. In sharp contrast to all failed attempts and empty sacrifices, Jesus performs only one act, offers a single sacrifice: himself. In that single, perfect sacrifice all former oft-repeated sacrifices are shown for what they truly are: failures. In place of the blood of animals there is the blood of Jesus, the blood which speaks mercy. Jesus is not only the perfect, holy and unspotted sacrifice, he is also the perfect sacrificer. Eternal priest, appointed so by oath of God, Jesus alone can make the perfect offering for sins.

Because he is both perfect sacrifice and perfect priest, Jesus attains that which has always been impossible: true forgiveness of sin and true reconciliation between God and his people. Having achieved true redemption on behalf of his sisters and brothers, Jesus continues his mediation. He intercedes for us, he is present with God, he is our way to our God. The one who believes in Jesus Christ is able now to come to God, to enter into his presence and there to find mercy and incredible joy. All of history is reversed in Jesus, all of the failures are overcome, all of the hopes and longings are fulfilled, for in Jesus the true mediator is finally and fully made present.

There are, then, numerous Christological titles in Hebrews, and multiple aspects to the Christology of the homily. When these are reviewed and seen in their interrelatedness, one can only respond with gratitude and, freed from sin, join with the community of the new covenant in their cry of faith in Jesus Christ Mediator. "Jesus Christ the same yesterday, and today, and for ever." (Heb 13:8)

CULTIC REGULATIONS.
9:1-10.

9 Now even the first covenant had regulations for worship and an earthly sanctuary. ²For a tent was prepared, the outer one, in which were the lampstand and the table and the bread of the Presence; it is called the Holy Place. ³Behind the second curtain stood a tent called the Holy of Holies, ⁴having the golden altar of incense and the ark of the covenant covered on all sides with gold, which contained a golden urn holding the manna, and Aaron's rod that budded, and the tables of the covenant; ⁵above it were the cherubim of glory overshadowing the mercy seat. Of these things we cannot now speak in detail.

⁶These preparations having thus been made, the priests go continually into the outer tent, performing their ritual duties; ⁷but into the second only the high priest goes, and he but once a year, and not without taking blood which he offers for himself and for the errors of the people. ⁸By this the Holy Spirit indicates that the way into the sanctuary is not yet opened as long as the outer tent is still standing ⁹(which is symbolic for the present age). According to this arrangement, gifts and sacrifices are offered which cannot perfect the conscience of the worshiper, ¹⁰but deal only with food and drink and various ablutions, regulations for the body imposed until the time of reformation.

Having established the necessity for a second and better covenant, the homilist returns now to the cultic institutions of the first covenant. While these verses may seem to be repetitious and a backward step, they are in fact very important as they enable our homilist to make very clear *why* the priesthood of Christ is the perfect one and why his sacrifice is the final one.

In 9:1-5 the homilist returns to the Old Testament descriptions, part of which he cited in 8:5. Here he concentrates upon the construction of the tent itself. The outer section of the tent contained the lamp stand and a table upon which was placed the "Bread of the Presence." This bread consisted of twelve loaves, replaced each week. It was called the Bread of the Presence because it was near to the inner sanctuary where the presence of God was believed to be.

The inner sanctuary, called the Holy of Holies, was separated from the outer by a veil and contained the Ark of the Covenant. The Ark held some of the manna, the food miraculously given by God in the desert; Aaron's staff, the symbol of his priesthood; and the tablets upon which were written the code of covenant (the Ten Commandments). At the top of the Ark were built two fiery-looking creatures, the cherubim. These were nothing like the cherubs one sees in much art, but were rather powerful creatures who were thought to accompany God in his appearances (see, for example, chapter 10 of Ezekiel). These cherubim guarded the mercy seat, the place where God came to rest when he entered the sanctuary. It was here, before the mercy seat, that one came into direct contact with God, that one stood before the presence of the Divine.

Verses 6-11 concentrate upon entrance to that presence. Priests went often into the outer tent, but only one person could enter the Holy of Holies and he could do so only once a year, on the Day of Atonement. The high priest entered the inner sanctuary only on this day, and sprinkled sacrificial blood upon the altar. He did so in order to make atonement for the holy place because of the sins of the people of Israel. In what follows, the homilist draws symbolic value from this ritual and passes judgement on it.

The existence of the two tents, and the limited access to the actual presence of God indicate that full, complete entrance into God's presence for all the people was not yet a reality. This fact is, further, symbolic of the present time. All cannot approach God directly. It is said that the Holy Spirit indicates this because, for our homilist, all words of the Old Testament were the Holy Spirit's words.

Not only did the construction of the tent point to limited ineffectual relationship with God, the rituals themselves were faulty. They were so because they were merely external rites and could not reach the interior, the heart (or conscience) of the individual. With this judgement, our homilist reaches a crucial point in his argument. For him the whole old covenant could not enable one to approach God. It was unable to do so because it could not attain forgiveness of sin. This forgiveness of sin, promised in the new covenant as seen in the text from Jeremiah 31, was impossible under the old law because it dealt only with externals. Under the old covenant, then, one is doomed to futility. There is a way out—a way *in*, really—and it is to this way that we turn now.

CHRIST, THE PERFECT HIGH PRIEST.
9:11-22.

> [11]But when Christ appeared as a high priest of the good things that have come, then through the greater and more perfect tent (not made with hands, that is, not of this creation) [12]he entered once for all into the Holy Place, taking not the blood of goats and calves but his own blood, thus securing an eternal redemption. [13]For if the sprinkling of defiled persons with the blood of goats and bulls and with the ashes of a heifer sanctifies for the purification of the flesh, [14]how much more shall the blood of Christ, who through the eternal Spirit offered himself without blemish to God, purify your conscience from dead works to serve the living God.
>
> [15]Therefore he is the mediator of a new covenant, so that those who are called may receive the promised eternal inheritance, since a death has occurred which redeems

them from the transgressions under the first covenant.
[16]For where a will is involved, the death of the one who
made it must be established. [17]For a will takes effect only
at death, since it is not in force as long as the one who
made it is alive. [18]Hence even the first covenant was not
ratified without blood. [19]For when every commandment
of the law had been declared by Moses to all the people,
he took the blood of calves and goats, with water and
scarlet wool and hyssop, and sprinkled both the book
itself and all the people, [20]saying, "This is the blood of
the covenant which God commanded you." [21]And in the
same way he sprinkled with blood both the tent and all
the vessels used in worship. [22]Indeed, under the law
almost everything is purified with blood, and without the
shedding of blood there is no forgiveness of sins.

We have now reached the exact center of this homily and
it is typical of the homilist's absolute concentration upon
Jesus Christ and his sacrifice that *the* center word of
Hebrews is, in fact, "Christ." In the Greek text the word
order is different than our English translation and "Christ"
stands in an emphatic position at the very beginning of the
verse. Whereas 8:1 seemed to call for a drum roll, "Christ"
in 9:11 evokes a cymbal crash, for he is the way, the *only*
way, out of the futility of unforgiven sin and ineffectual
rite. Verses 11-14 show how this is true, and 15-22 show what
Christ's sacrifice effects.

This perfect sacrifice is now compared with the previous
inadequate old covenant sacrifices. Christ is high priest of
the "good things that have come." This expression, a technical one, points to the fact that in Jesus' ministry the new,
eschatological age has begun. Christ has entered not merely
the inner sanctuary of the tent, but the truly holy place, the
dwelling place of God. Here in verse 11 the homilist refers
back to the reference to the copy of the heavenly sanctuary
in 8:5. Whereas multiple high priests entered the inner
sanctuaries many times over the years, Christ enters the
perfect sanctuary once and only once. While they offered

the blood of sacrificial animals, Jesus offered his own blood. His blood, that is, his sacrifice of himself, effects what the blood of animals could not do. It attains eternal redemption.

The homilist employs a comparative argument again to illustrate how much greater is the sacrifice of Jesus Christ. If the old covenant sacrifices, ineffectual as they were, were yet able to attain external purification, then certainly the perfect sacrifice of the Christ is able to achieve perfect purification, purification of the conscience. Here, in these few verses, we have a unique statement of the meaning of the Christ-event. We have, further, a summary statement of the point of the entire homily. Jesus Christ, in his sacrifice of himself, has done what never could be accomplished before. He has secured eternal redemption for his people. This redemption is described as purification of the conscience in direct contrast to 9:9. Such purification implies more than a feeling, or an intuition that one is no longer guilty, it implies service of the living God. The christian believer turns from slavery to a law and to sacrifice which did not work. This believer is now freed by Christ's unique sacrifice to serve the God who lives.

This is why Jesus is the perfect and the *only* high priest. He has done what no former priest could do. This is why his is the perfect sacrifice. It has done what no other sacrifice could do. This is, as the following verses will show, why Jesus is the mediator of the promised new covenant. For only he could bring about the conditions necessary for its establishment.

The sins of the first covenant had necessarily to be forgiven: "And I will remember their sins no more." (Heb 8:12=Jer 31:34). Jesus' death brought about that forgiveness and hence enabled those called by God to receive the inheritance that was theirs. The reference to death and inheritance leads our homilist to use an example from civil law, and to employ a play on word-meanings. The original Greek word for covenant can also mean 'testament' in the sense of "last will and testament." It is this sense which our homilist uses now. Since a last will and testament becomes effective only upon the death of the testator, the death of Jesus was necessary to bring the will/covenant into effect.

The homilist returns to the idea of covenant and once again compares the old covenant and the new, this time in terms of the institution of the covenant. The ceremony described in Exodus 24:6-8 is referred to, particularly the use of blood in the establishment of the covenant. The sprinkling of the blood of a sacrificed animal was symbolic of the purification attained by the sacrifice. Because blood was considered to be the life force in a living being, it was seen as effective in attaining forgiveness of sins. The homilist concludes this old covenant reference with a general statement: there is no forgiveness without the shedding of blood. The old covenant institution rite serves as example of the necessity for the shedding of blood for the forgiveness of sins. The unspoken conclusion is "hence, the absolute necessity for the shedding of Jesus' blood."

CHRIST: THE PERFECT SACRIFICE.
9:23-28.

> [23]Thus it was necessary for the copies of the heavenly things to be purified with these rites, but the heavenly things themselves with better sacrifices than these. [24]For Christ has entered, not into a sanctuary made with hands, a copy of the true one, but into heaven itself, now to appear in the presence of God on our behalf. [25]Nor was it to offer himself repeatedly, as the high priest enters the Holy Place yearly with blood not his own; [26]for then he would have had to suffer repeatedly since the foundation of the world. But as it is, he has appeared once for all at the end of the age to put away sin by the sacrifice of himself. [27]And just as it is appointed for men to die once, and after that comes judgment, [28]so Christ, having been offered once to bear the sins of many, will appear a second time, not to deal with sin but to save those who are eagerly waiting for him.

The homilist returns now to concentrate upon the sacrifice of Christ itself. His transitional sentence (in vs. 23) speaks of the necessity of greater sacrifices for true purification. The language in this verse seems to posit a kind of dualism common to the ancient world. The verse refers to "copies of heavenly things" and to "heavenly things themselves" and could imply that the "earthly copies" were not *real* but merely images and shadows (see 8:5, 10:1) of the true reality which is heavenly. For many scholars, this verse is typical of a dualism which posits an unbridgeable gap between heaven and earth. The heavenly, eternal, spiritual elements are the only truly real ones while the earthly, temporal, physical aspects are but shadows. The earthly is doomed to destruction so that the heavenly may be released. This kind of thinking emanated primarily from the Greek world and ultimately resulted in a gnosticism (from *gnosis* = knowledge) which, among other things, denied any validity or value to the concrete earthly reality. For some, our homilist belongs to that world of thought.

It must be acknowledged that Hebrews does contain the language of a dualistic system. Undoubtedly our homilist was acquainted with such a system and made use of its vocabulary. We should not be too quick to consider him as a "dualist," however, for the image of the heavenly temple and heavenly dwelling place was also a Judaic one, and the reference to the true Holy of Holies originated in a citation of an Old Testament text in 8:5-6. "Heavenly" can refer to either the eternal, spiritual realm as opposed to the temporal, physical reality, or to the place where God is. It is this author's opinion that our homilist employs the latter meaning. For him, the drama of salvation focuses upon the possibility/impossibility of approach to God. In order to make it clear that Jesus' sacrifice has finally made such approach possible, he uses imagery related to heaven and the heavenly, because that is where God is.

It is into this heavenly realm that Christ has entered in order to intercede for us. He has not done this repeatedly as did the high priest of the old covenant. He has sacrificed himself once and only once and has put away sin. He has appeared "at the end of the age," that is, at the end of the old age, the ineffective age when sin still barred humankind's access to God. With the sacrifice of Christ, the *new* age, the age of fulfillment has begun. *This* age, while begun, still awaits the final consummation which will take place when Jesus returns. His return will not be to deal with sin for he has done that once and for all just as one dies only once. It will, rather, be a time when Jesus will save those who await him. In these verses our homilist employs the classic New Testament eschatological schema: in Jesus the old age has ended and the new, final days have begun; these final days will have their ultimate consummation in the glorious return of the Risen Christ. The "Hebrews" live in the time of the new covenant but they also live as those waiting upon the Lord.

SINGLE OFFERING, ETERNAL SALVATION. 10:1-18.

10   For since the law has but a shadow of the good things to come instead of the true form of these realities, it can never, by the same sacrifices which are continually offered year after year, make perfect those who draw near. ²Otherwise, would they not have ceased to be offered? If the worshipers had once been cleansed, they would no longer have any consciousness of sin. ³But in these sacrifices there is a reminder of sin year after year. ⁴For it is impossible that the blood of bulls and goats should take away sins.

⁵Consequently, when Christ came into the world, he said,

"Sacrifices and offerings thou hast not desired,
  but a body hast thou prepared for me;
⁶in burnt offerings and sin offerings thou hast
    taken no pleasure.
⁷Then I said, 'Lo, I have come to do thy will, O God,'
  as it is written of me in the roll of the book."
⁸When he said above, "Thou hast neither desired nor taken pleasure in sacrifices and offerings and burnt

offerings and sin offerings (these are offered according to the law), [9]then he added, "Lo, I have come to do thy will." He abolishes the first in order to establish the second. [10]And by that will we have been sanctified through the offering of the body of Jesus Christ once for all.

[11]And every priest stands daily at his service, offering repeatedly the same sacrifices, which can never take away sins. [12]But when Christ had offered for all time a single sacrifice for sins, he sat down at the right hand of God, [13]then to wait until his enemies should be made a stool for his feet. [14]For by a single offering he has perfected for all time those who are sanctified. [15]And the Holy Spirit also bears witness to us; for after saying,

[16]"This is the covenant that I will make with them
after those days, says the Lord:
I will put my laws on their hearts,
and write them on their minds,"
[17]then he adds,
"I will remember their sins and their misdeeds no more."
[18]Where there is forgiveness of these, there is no longer any offering for sin.

The first section of chapter 10 contains a final comparison between the old covenant sacrifices and that of Jesus. It also draws a further and most important conclusion: sacrifice for sin is over. The saving act of Jesus has wiped out any need for further sacrifice.

The homilist begins with another statement which employs technical dualistic vocabulary. The law (the law governing cultic institutions such as sacrifices and sin offerings) is only the 'shadow' of the 'true form' of the good things to come. One can understand this to mean that the old covenant realities were not truly real but were merely copies of the heavenly reality. The inferior earthly was to be replaced by the eternal heavenly. In this same verse, the homilist speaks of the "good things to come." This expression is also a technical one, but it comes from another, different mode of thought: one that is primarily Judaic and eschatological. As Israel lived in hope of the promises of

God, as they looked forward to that time when they would finally receive the inheritance, so too they waited for the "good things to come." Christian thought quickly adopted this type of expression, with one radical change. The promises, the good things to come, were already here. In Jesus' act, the future age had already begun. One waited then (and still waits) for the consummation of this future in the second coming of the Risen Christ.

We have seen that all of these ideas are present in Hebrews. Promise is central to our homilist, as is inheritance. The last verse of chapter 9 speaks, as we have just seen, of the second coming of Christ. The first verse of chapter 10, which follows immediately upon this clearly eschatological promise of the preceding sentence, which posits a shadow/reality dualism, which nonetheless contains Judaic eschatological terminology, is typical of our homilist. Both types of thought and both modes of expression are used in Hebrews. Our homilist was undoubtedly a gifted person who was capable of adapting many prevailing currents of thought and language in order to make the point, to move the hearers to faith and endurance.

In our culture today we sometimes encounter a gifted orator who is able to speak to people in their own language: the professor who can communicate in "street talk," the American diplomat capable of thinking in the cultural milieu of another country, the parent who really understands the language of children. All of these individuals are exceptional because they are able to communicate with others in language, which carries not only words, but emotions and memories significant for people. Our homilist is such an individual. While Hebrews may not evoke *our* emotions and memories with all of its discussion of cult and sacrifice, it certainly would have moved the community of the "Hebrews." We must keep in mind that the homilist is addressing people whose lives were deeply involved in and influenced by these institutions, and that he is telling them they must not return to them.

Events in recent Roman Catholic life provide us with a rather apt parallel. For those Catholics who truly loved the Latin liturgy with its sense of mystery and beauty, its lofty chants and pageantry, liturgical reform was less than a boon. English replaced Latin, guitar and folk music were substituted for Gregorian chant, peace greetings took the place of genuflections and blessings. The people were asked to turn from something very rich, very old, very moving and to worship in a less emotionally satisfying way. *And,* many people have done so with regret, with longing for the "old ways"; many, too, have returned to that former, more elaborate way.

So too the "Hebrews." They are asked to turn from their own rich and mysterious cultic heritage and to remain faithful to a new way, a way less satisfying and much less secure. This new way no longer entails sacrifices, high priests, or external ritual seen to effect purification over and over again. Instead, the homilist says, christian life demands conversion, confidence and—above all—faith. The burden is placed upon the believer now, not on the ritual. This is a stark and rather frightening way to live religiously, but it is the only way for our homilist. "You cannot go back," he cries, "if you do you are lost!" There is only one direction: forward, approach to God. Small wonder he uses any means possible to convince his hearers *and* to give them confidence.

The failure of the old cultic institutions are stressed again in 10:1-4. The law could never free the worshippers from sin. Those who approached God could never actually do so for they could never be forgiven their sin. It is significant to note that perfection is typically described here as purification of sin and the ability to approach God. Not only were the old laws unable to effect such perfection, they actually served as a constant reminder that sin existed. Every time the people sought atonement they were made conscious that they *needed* atonement. The sacrificial blood could not purify, only remind. Here the homilist draws upon all that has been said about the significance of blood sacrifices and of the Old Testament offerings, especially that of the Day of Atonement. He goes one step further, however. Not only is it impossible for the blood of bulls and goats to take away sins (see 9:13), these very sacrifices continually remind the sinners of this fact.

But, with Christ, all is changed. The external, ineffectual offerings are replaced by the obedient self-offering of Jesus. The homilist quotes Psalm 40:6-8 and attributes it to Christ himself. These Psalm verses are taken as an indication that the old covenant sacrifices were worthless and were to be replaced by the obedient servant, come to obey the will of God. In his commentary on the text, the homilist says that Christ has abolished the first (the old covenant institution) and has established the second (the new covenant). He has done so by his obedience to God's will which decreed our sanctification through the single, perfect sacrifice of Jesus Christ.

The homilist reinforces his argument with a reference to one element of the cultic action. Whereas the priest continuously offers and continuously adopts the stance of offering and petition (standing), Christ has offered once and has since ceased to stand but has taken the position of authority: he is seated. Further, he is seated at the right hand of God. His sacrifice finished, he takes his rightful place where he awaits the final consummation of the age. For in one offering, one fully obedient act, he has made perfect *forever* all those whose sin has been forgiven.

He has established the promised new covenant. Here the homilist once again cites the Jeremiah prophecy. As Christ has borne witness to his own ministry in 9:5-9, now too the Spirit testifies to this ministry. The whole text of the prophecy is not repeated here as it was in 8:8-12. Although only two verses are cited, they are both very significant. The first is the introduction to the prophecy and serves to recall the whole promise. The second (vs. 17) is the more important and stresses that *the* point of the new covenant is the forgiveness of sin. According to our homilist, the unattainable has been given, sin has been forgiven, the new covenant is now in effect. The last verse of this section draws a logical but also radical conclusion. There is no more sacrifice for sins. That is, the entire cultic sacrificial fabric of life under the first covenant is wiped out. One can almost feel the hearers wince as they hear of the demolishment of their former life.

Hebrews has traditionally been called the "Epistle of Priesthood." In one sense, the title is a very apt one, in another, it is a misnomer. The title is correct if we are talking about the ministry of Jesus. Jesus is clearly depicted as *the* great high priest, especially as his ministry contrasts with the ineffectual Levitical priesthood. As the offering of sacrifice has come to an end with the forgiveness attained in Jesus' sacrifice, so too has the priesthood which was responsible for the former offerings. Jesus is the perfect—and the final— high priest.

When the references to priesthood are applied to the contemporary Roman Catholic priesthood, they are done so incorrectly, for two main reasons. In the first place, two kinds of priesthood are spoken of in Hebrews: the priesthood which was faulty and which was abolished (10:8-9); the perfect priesthood of Jesus which is by its very nature unique and unrepeatable. There is no idea in Hebrews of a continuation of Jesus' priesthood in any members of the community. This was not a concern of our homilist. In the second place, the office of priest as we know it now did not exist in the early christian communities. It is, therefore, beyond (and perhaps contrary to) the homilist's intention to apply statements about priesthood in Hebrews to priests of the contemporary church. This is not to deny the validity of priesthood, it is merely to say that Hebrews is not the place where such priesthood is described.

ENCOURAGEMENT, WARNING.
10:19-39.

[19]Therefore, brethren, since we have confidence to enter the sanctuary by the blood of Jesus, [20]by the new

and living way which he opened for us through the curtain, that is, through his flesh, [21]and since we have a great priest over the house of God, [22]let us draw near with a true heart in full assurance of faith, with our hearts sprinkled clean from an evil conscience and our bodies washed with pure water. [23]Let us hold fast the confession of our hope without wavering, for he who promised is faithful; [24]and let us consider how to stir up one another to love and good works, [25]not neglecting to meet together, as is the habit of some, but encouraging one another, and all the more as you see the Day drawing near.

[26]For if we sin deliberately after receiving the knowledge of the truth, there no longer remains a sacrifice for sins, [27]but a fearful prospect of judgment, and a fury of fire which will consume the adversaries. [28]A man who has violated the law of Moses dies without mercy at the testimony of two or three witnesses. [29]How much worse punishment do you think will be deserved by the man who has spurned the Son of God, and profaned the blood of the covenant by which he was sanctified, and outraged the spirit of grace? [30]For we know him who said, "Vengeance is mine, I will repay." And again, "The Lord will judge his people." [31]It is a fearful thing to fall into the hands of the living God.

[32]But recall the former days when, after you were enlightened, you endured a hard struggle with sufferings, [33]sometimes being publicly exposed to abuse and affliction, and sometimes being partners with those so treated. [34]For you had compassion on the prisoners, and you joyfully accepted the plundering of your property, since you knew that you yourselves had a better possession and an abiding one. [35]Therefore do not throw away your confidence, which has a great reward. [36]For you have need of endurance, so that you may do the will of God and receive what is promised.

[37]"For yet a little while,
    and the coming one shall come and shall not tarry;

> 38but my righteous one shall live by faith,
>   and if he shrinks back,
>   my soul has no pleasure in him."
> 39But we are not of those who shrink back and are destroyed, but of those who have faith and keep their souls.

Having made the point that all is finally forgiven, that Jesus' sacrifice has abolished all former sacrifices and has enabled believers to approach the face of God, the homilist turns now to the community and involves them in this reality. We have reached the end of the central section of Hebrews. The homilist repeats the method used at the beginning of the section (5:11 – 6:12): he addresses the "Hebrews" directly, refers to their actual situation, exhorts them, encourages them and warns them. In 10:19-25 the community is exhorted to fidelity, in 26-31 they are warned, (menaced, one might say!), in 32-39 they are encouraged.

Verses 19-25 are one sentence. The RSV has added the period in verse 22! This sentence, which portrays the meaning and the mission involved in all that has gone before, contains three exhortations: let us approach (vs. 22), let us hold fast (vs. 23), let us exhort one another (vs. 24). The first is the direct consequence of the fact that we have been enabled to approach. The second applies to the situation in which the "Hebrews" stand at the moment (this exhortation will be elaborated in vss. 26-31). The third introduces the members' responsibilities for each other. Christianity is not an individualistic way of life for our homilist. This exhortation is expanded in verses 32-39.

We must approach God because we are able to do so. We can now enter into the true sanctuary with confidence. We can do so because Jesus, pioneer of salvation (2:10) has opened the way for us. This way has been opened by the sacrifice of Jesus which has penetrated through the curtain that separated the people from the presence of God. The Greek text is somewhat ambiguous here and it is not clear if "flesh" refers to the curtain (i.e., his flesh was the curtain) or to the way (i.e., he went through the curtain in his flesh). In either case, the homilist makes the point that, in his flesh and blood sacrifice, Jesus has broken down all barriers between humanity and God. Where before only the high priest entered once a year and then did so to no avail, now *all* enter and do so confidently and effectively. In language very similar to 4:14-16, the homilist once again reminds the community that they have a great high priest over them, for they are the house of God (see 3:6-7). They can, therefore, approach God with a true heart—one freed from the deceit of sin and confident in faith. Grounded in faith in Jesus, they have no need to hesitate, to pause, to ask, "Are you sure I belong here?" They draw near as those whose hearts have finally been purified (they no longer have consciousness of sin: 10:2-3), and, perhaps, as those who have sealed their faith in baptism ("our bodies washed with pure water vs. 22).

The believers must hold firmly to belief and the hope to which it gives rise. This is, of course, the key exhortation in Hebrews. In face of a tendency to return to the old and the comfortable, the "Hebrews" are urged to hang on to the treasure they have been given. The reason for such endurance is significant: *God* is faithful. The homilist does not lay all the burden upon his people and their willpower. Rather, he shows them what it is that enables them to continue, the fidelity of the one who has promised. We have seen, especially in 6:13-20, how *sure* is the promise of God.

Finally, the community members are to support and minister to each other. The homilist wisely recognizes that the preacher is not solely responsible for the faith-life of the community. This exhortation offers another clue to the life situation of the "Hebrews." Apparently some were withdrawing from the community worship, perhaps those who had succumbed to the lure of former ritual. The "Hebrews" must encourage one another in their fidelity. The homilist injects a note of urgency here for he speaks of the Day which is drawing near. This Day, the final day of judgment, reminds the hearers that there is, indeed, a day of reckoning before them. . . and that it is coming soon.

The mention of the Day in verse 25 leads the homilist to speak a warning—one even more threatening than that of 6:4-8. In this warning what is in store for one who does not hold fast is depicted in all its frightening reality. Hebrews 10:26-31 resembles 6:4-8 very closely. Both speak of the christian initiation and of rejection of the christian experience. Both, finally, promise total condemnation for the one who rejects the good news of God's salvation in Jesus Christ. Hebrews 10:26-31 is a more dreadful warning, however, since it follows after the homilist's exposition of the saving effect of Christ's one-time sacrifice and builds upon that presentation.

When he begins by speaking of "sinning deliberately," the homilist is not talking about a "deliberate sin," but rather of the complete and total rejection of something one has known, and known experientially. If you reject what has been given to you, he says, there is no recourse. Since the perfect sacrifice has been made once-for-all, there can be no other sacrifice for sins. There is one way and one way only to know forgiveness, and if that way is rejected no other possibility exists. What does exist is living in fear of certain judgment and facing the eschatological fire that will destroy.

In order to strengthen his argument, the homilist uses his favorite method of comparing an Old Testament reality to that of the New. Here he refers to the Old Testament law which declared that one who had turned from worship of the God of Israel was to be stoned to death upon the testimony of two or three witnesses (Deut 17:2-6). The homilist adds the phrase "without mercy" (vs. 28) in order to stress the terrible, inescapable fate which awaited such a sinner. If death awaited those who sinned against the old, less important covenant, what can be expected for those who reject the new? This rejection is given a graphic description which stresses the majesty of Jesus (the Son of God), recalls all that has been said of the meaning of the sacrifice and blood of the Christ, and speaks of outraging the spirit of grace. What shall become of one who has spurned and despised the glorious reality that the homilist has so painstakingly presented in the preceding chapters, *and* that the sinner himself/herself has known and experienced?

The Old Testament once again supplies an answer. Here the homilist cites Deuteronomy 32:35-36 where God's vengeance and judgment are promised. God himself has spoken these words and God himself will repay the apostate. It is not surprising that the homilist concludes this warning by stressing the fearsomeness of encounter with the living (judging) God.

Obviously the homilist does not intend that the message he speaks should lead to complacency. He does tell us, as he has done in 6:4-8, that for those who reject totally the reality that is the new covenant, no second chance is possible. At the same time, the homilist does not seek to panic the listeners or to plunge them into despair. This *can* happen, we are told; we are not told, however, that it *has* happened.

Having evoked this fearful menace, the homilist now turns once again to encouragement. He recalls the beginning days of their faith, when they were "enlightened" (see 6:4). The "Hebrews" are to remember their fidelity in times of suffering and to take strength from what they were able to endure. Further indications of the situation of the mysterious "Hebrews" are given in these verses. They have known some persecution and have had property taken from them. They are, then, "seasoned" Christians, who have lived beyond those first glorious days of rebirth. More importantly, they successfully held on to their belief in the difficult times. They did so because they knew the value of what they possessed as believers. It is this fidelity which allows the homilist to urge them to continue until they have received the fullness of God's promise. You have done so well, don't give up now!

An Old Testament citation is used again, one which aptly sums up both aspects of the exhortation. Habakkuk 2:3-4 is cited (in reverse order) to remind the community members that judgment is coming soon (see 10:25) and to urge them to fidelity rather than to giving up or "shrinking back." The final verse of the chapter stands for all time as a description of the true Christian. Two options are given here: retreat and destruction; fidelity and salvation. There is, as we have been so clearly shown, no alternative. The "Hebrews" are among those who have chosen the latter option. Chapter eleven will recall for them (and for us) the many others who have also lived in patient faith.

IV. THE RIGHTEOUS ONES WHO LIVE BY FAITH.
11:1 – 12:13

In this section the homilist presents examples of those who did not shrink back, as he has said in 10:38-39. He also offers a reflection on the meaning of faith. He does this both in terms of the lives of the individuals he names and in terms of his own comments about faith. Chapter 11 can be seen as a history of God's people from the point of view of their belief in God, and especially in his promises. It is one of the more well-known texts in Hebrews and one dominated by the refrain-like expression "by faith" (see vss. 3, 4, 5, 8, 9, 11, 17, 20, 21, 23, 24, 27, 28, 29, 31). The great Old Testament models of faith lead our homilist to exhort the New Testament believers to run the race set before them in 12:1-13.

THE STORY OF FAITH, PART ONE.
11:1-16.

> **11** Now faith is the assurance of things hoped for, the conviction of things not seen. ²For by it the men of old received divine approval. ³By faith we understand that the world was created by the word of God, so that what is seen was made out of things which do not appear.
>
> ⁴By faith Abel offered to God a more acceptable sacrifice than Cain, through which he received approval as righteous, God bearing witness by accepting his gifts; he

died, but through his faith he is still speaking. ⁵By faith Enoch was taken up so that he should not see death; and he was not found, because God had taken him. Now before he was taken he was attested as having pleased God. ⁶And without faith it is impossible to please him. For whoever would draw near to God must believe that he exists and that he rewards those who seek him. ⁷By faith Noah, being warned by God concerning events as yet unseen, took heed and constructed an ark for the saving of his household; by this he condemned the world and became an heir of the righteousness which comes by faith.

⁸By faith Abraham obeyed when he was called to go out to a place which he was to receive as an inheritance; and he went out, not knowing where he was to go. ⁹By faith he sojourned in the land of promise, as in a foreign land, living in tents with Isaac and Jacob, heirs with him of the same promise. ¹⁰For he looked forward to the city which has foundations, whose builder and maker is God. ¹¹By faith Sarah herself received power to conceive, even when she was past the age, since she considered him faithful who had promised. ¹²Therefore from one man, and him as good as dead, were born descendants as many as the stars of heaven and as the innumerable grains of sand by the seashore.

¹³These all died in faith, not having received what was promised, but having seen it and greeted it from afar, and having acknowledged that they were strangers and exiles on earth. ¹⁴For people who speak thus make it clear that they are seeking a homeland. ¹⁵If they had been thinking of that land from which they had gone out, they would have had opportunity to return. ¹⁶But as it is, they desire a better country, that is, a heavenly one. Therefore God is not ashamed to be called their God, for he has prepared for them a city.

The homilist defines faith in a two-fold way. First, it is "the assurance of things hoped for." In other words, it is the inner guarantee one has that what stands in the future will indeed be as God has promised. Second, faith is the conviction of things not seen, that is, faith is the certainty that what is neither present nor visible does, in fact, exist. What cannot be grasped is nonetheless real. The homilist's definition is a *stark* one for it implies that one has nothing upon which to rest one's faith save God's word. This implication becomes more and more explicit as the list of believers progresses. For now the homilist states only that such faith gained approval from God.

The "story of faith" begins with creation itself, for faith is required to recognize that the mighty word of God did indeed create the visible world from things which cannot be seen. "Faith is the conviction of things not seen. . ." The first of the faithful is Abel, who, by faith, made acceptable sacrifice to God. The homilist refers here to the story of Cain and Abel (Gen 4:3-10) wherein Abel, having offered acceptable sacrifice, was blessed by God. Cain's offering was not accepted, and in anger and jealousy Cain murdered his brother Abel. The Old Testament text tells us that the blood of Abel cried out to God, and that God placed a curse on Cain. Our homilist interprets this story to mean that because of Abel's faith he made the acceptable sacrifice, and also because of his faith, his blood not only cried out then but continues to do so. The homilist will make very effective use of this fact in 12:24 where he compares Abel's blood and that of Jesus.

The second example is Enoch (Gen 5:21-24). Enoch, we are told, "walked with God." At the age of 365, God "took" Enoch, thus he never suffered death. Enoch's goodness and his escape from death are attributed to his faith. The statement that Enoch pleased God (as well as the citation of Hab 2:3 in 10:38) leads our homilist to an important lesson concerning the necessity of faith. Without it, it is *impossible* to please God. Anyone who would seek to approach God must believe. The word used for "approach" in 11:6 is the same cultic expression used before. When he says one must believe in God in order to approach him, the homilist is speaking of the same people whom he has just urged to "approach with a true heart in full assurance of faith." (10:22, see also 4:14-16). One must believe not only that God is, but that he also is the *living* God and that he responds to those who seek him. Faith, then, is prerequisite and means to entrance into relationship with God.

The next person named is Noah. Noah believed the word of God concerning things unseen and obeyed God's word (Gen 6:13-22). Because he believed Noah became an heir of the righteousness of faith. "My righteous one shall live by faith." (10:38; Hab 2:3). He and his household were saved while the rest of the world perished.

The homilist turns now to Abraham and Sarah. Abraham is a prime example for two reasons: he believed the promise of God, and journeyed to an unknown land. The promise made to Abraham was introduced in 6:13 and will continue to be developed here. The unknown land or city will become a significant concept in chapters 12 and 13. Abraham believed and obeyed the call to enter a strange land. Once in that land, neither Abraham nor his sons Isaac and Jacob took possession of it. They still looked forward to another city—one built by God, as was the true tent in 8:2.

Sarah, too, believed in God's promise and thus was able to conceive. Because she believed, their descendants were as numerous as "stars in heaven" or "grains of sand." Here the homilist makes allusion to the promise of God as given in Genesis 32:12.

While Abraham did become father of innumerable descendants, he did not really receive the full promise of God. The important point for our homilist is that Abraham, Sarah, Isaac, and Jacob left their homeland and never turned back. At the word of God they moved forward into the unknown, dwelt in the land as exiles. They sought for a better country, a heavenly one; and, because they believed, God is not ashamed to be called their God. Here we recall Hebrews 2:11 where it was said that Jesus is not ashamed to call us sister and brother. God has, in fact, prepared a city for these believers, one which they saw only from afar but which the Christian is able to enter (as 12:22-24 will show).

THE STORY OF FAITH, PART TWO.
11:17-40.

[17]By faith Abraham, when he was tested, offered up Isaac, and he who had received the promises was ready to offer up his only son, [18]of whom it was said, "Through Isaac shall your descendants be named." [19]He considered that God was able to raise men even from the dead; hence, figuratively speaking, he did receive him back. [20]By faith Isaac invoked future blessings on Jacob and Esau. [21]By faith Jacob, when dying, blessed each of the sons of Joseph, bowing in worship over the head of his staff. [22]By faith Joseph, at the end of his life, made mention of the exodus of the Israelites and gave directions concerning his burial.

[23]By faith Moses, when he was born, was hid for three months by his parents, because they saw that the child was beautiful; and they were not afraid of the king's edict. [24]By faith Moses, when he was grown up, refused to be called the son of Pharaoh's daughter, [25]choosing rather to share ill-treatment with the people of God than to enjoy the fleeting pleasures of sin. [26]He considered abuse suffered for the Christ greater wealth than the treasures of Egypt, for he looked to the reward. [27]By faith he left Egypt, not being afraid of the anger of the king; for he endured as seeing him who is invisible. [28]By faith he kept the Passover and sprinkled the blood, so that the Destroyer of the first-born might not touch them.

[29]By faith the people crossed the Red Sea as if on dry land; but the Egyptians, when they attempted to do the same, were drowned. [30]By faith the walls of Jericho fell down after they had been encircled for seven days. [31]By faith Rahab the harlot did not perish with those who were

disobedient, because she had given friendly welcome to the spies.

32And what more shall I say? For time would fail me to tell of Gideon, Barak, Samson, Jephthah, of David and Samuel and the prophets—33who through faith conquered kingdoms, enforced justice, received promises, stopped the mouths of lions, 34quenched raging fire, escaped the edge of the sword, won strength out of weakness, became mighty in war, put foreign armies to flight. 35Women received their dead by resurrection. Some were tortured, refusing to accept release, that they might rise again to a better life. 36Others suffered mocking and scourging, and even chains and imprisonment. 37They were stoned, they were sawn in two, they were killed with the sword; they went about in skins of sheep and goats, destitute, afflicted, ill-treated—38of whom the world was not worthy—wandering over deserts and mountains, and in dens and caves of the earth.

39And all these, though well attested by their faith, did not receive what was promised, 40since God had foreseen something better for us, that apart from us they should not be made perfect.

The homilist now recounts the history of the people of Israel by means of the faith of their great heroes. He begins with Abraham's willingness to sacrifice Isaac, a willingness to destroy that part of the promise which he had received. Isaac, Jacob, and Joseph are also recalled. Moses, too, is seen to evidence faith throughout his life. In the case of Moses, the homilist's freedom with the Old Testament becomes manifest once again. The Old Testament accounts say nothing of Moses' refusal to be called Pharaoh's son, nor do they tell us that Moses was not afraid of Pharaoh's anger when he left Egypt. Exodus 2:14, in fact, says "Moses was afraid." Further, the homilist tells us that Moses chose to share the ill-treatment of Christ (vs. 26). The use of Christ is somewhat jarring here and looks at first as if the homilist assumes that Moses knew Christ. More likely the broader meaning of "God's anointed" is meant here. Moses preferred to share in the reproach suffered by God's anointed (or his anointed people) than to have the riches of Egypt.

The homilist sees important lessons in the life of Moses. He was one who—like Abraham—left his homeland, surrendered security and suffered because he believed the word of God. By faith, Moses looked forward to the as yet unrealized, and looked beyond the visible to the unseen.

Verses 29-38 trace the history of faith through the Exodus (29-31), the various heroes and heroines of the Old Testament and their great sufferings (32-38). It is worth noting here that, for our homilist, women were among the great witnesses of faith, and were seen to be equal in belief. Having listed the great deeds of faith, the risks involved, the sufferings endured, the story ends with a shock. Even with all their great faith, these persons did not receive the promise! Something more than faith is demanded it would seem: God's decision. God has decided upon something better for the christian community, and until this has been given, the Old Testament believers cannot be perfected.

What is this something better? Undoubtedly it is the new, better covenant (7:23) established upon better promises (8:6), a better hope (7:19). Ultimately it is the forgiveness of sin attained in the establishment of the new covenant. Perfection is closely allied with sanctification in Hebrews, and with approach to God. As we have seen, such approach was impossible before the saving sacrifice of Jesus. Even the Old Testament persons of faith could not receive the promise until the advent of the Christ. The giftedness of the christian reality stands in the background here. . . as cause for wonder.

RUN WITH PERSEVERANCE.
12:1-13.

> **12** Therefore, since we are surrounded by so great a cloud of witnesses, let us also lay aside every weight, and sin which clings so closely, and let us run with perseverance the race that is set before us, [2]looking to Jesus the

pioneer and perfecter of our faith, who for the joy that was set before him endured the cross, despising the shame, and is seated at the right hand of the throne of God.

[3]Consider him who endured from sinners such hostility against himself, so that you may not grow weary or faint-hearted. [4]In your struggle against sin you have not yet resisted to the point of shedding your blood. [5]And have you forgotten the exhortation which addresses you as sons?—

"My son, do not regard lightly the
    discipline of the Lord,
nor lose courage when you are
    punished by him.
[6]For the Lord disciplines him whom
    he loves,
and chastises every son whom he
    receives."

[7]It is for discipline that you have to endure. God is treating you as sons; for what son is there whom his father does not discipline? [8]If you are left without discipline, in which all have participated, then you are illegitimate children and not sons. [9]Besides this, we have had earthly fathers to discipline us and we respected them. Shall we not much more be subject to the Father of spirits and live? [10]For they disciplined us for a short time at their pleasure, but he disciplines us for our good, that we may share his holiness. [11]For the moment all discipline seems painful rather than pleasant; later it yields the peaceful fruit of righteousness to those who have been trained by it.

[12]Therefore lift your drooping hands and strengthen your weak knees, [13]and make straight paths for your feet, so that what is lame may not be put out of joint but rather be healed.

As he has done in 10:19-25, the homilist turns now to exhort the community in face of the series of examples he has just presented. Therefore. . . let *us*. . . This exhortation is to endurance and perseverance, as were all the others. It also leads to a warning as the others have done. The increase in urgency noted in the progressive exhortations is also to be found here. Hebrews 12:1-13 is dominated by the image of a race; the "Hebrews" must not merely persevere, they must *run* toward their goal! The warning which follows in 12:14-17 is the most concrete and the most terrible of any we have yet seen. Our homilist does not allow his listeners to relax.

Since we have so many examples of those who lived by faith, let us join the race, we are told. As a runner in a race removes everything which could weight him/her down, so too the Christian. It is interesting to note that sin is mentioned as one of the weights which must be removed. We have here an example of the realism of New Testament Christianity. Sin, the barrier which kept humankind from God, has been destroyed; there can be no doubt about that. Nonetheless, people still sin, still fail, still recreate their own barriers, reconstruct the veils. The weight of such sin slows down the Christian and makes her/him unable to persevere in the race.

The homilist turns the community's vision now, from the Old Testament witnesses to Jesus himself. Hebrews 12:2-3 remind us of the beginning chapters with their focus upon the person of Jesus and upon his mission. "Look to Jesus," we are told, "keep your eyes fastened on this one." Jesus is here called the pioneer and perfecter of our faith. He is both of these because, in his suffering, he both opened the way for our faith and brought it to fulfillment. Hebrews 2:10 calls Jesus the pioneer of our salvation who was himself brought to fulfillment through suffering. Here the homilist goes a step further: Jesus is pioneer who now brings others to fulfillment.

Jesus endured the cross, as we are to endure the race. The same word is used in both cases. As Jesus went beyond the cross and the shame of death as a criminal to attain glory as the Son of God seated at the right hand (Ps 110:1 is alluded to again), so too the Christian must persevere in order to attain fulness of salvation. The parallel between Jesus and the Christian continues in terms of the sufferings of the community in their present situation. They have apparently known some hardship and threats (see 10:32-35), but have not yet known an actual bloody persecution. If the phrase "struggle against sin" refers to battling against hostility, we have an indication that Hebrews was delivered before any of the general persecutions recorded in history. This would allow us to date it before that of Nero in 64 A.D. and certainly before the Domitian persecution at 90 A.D. Such datings must remain in the realm of theory, however.

Once again the homilist draws upon the Old Testament as resource. This time the citation is from Proverbs 3:11-12. While there is no commentary on the text, the quotation serves to introduce the idea of discipline as a reason for endurance. "It is for discipline that you have to endure." The image now moves to that of a father who disciplines his children. As a father so treats only his real children, so too *the* Father disciplines only *his* true children in order that they may share in his holiness.

The homilist is very human here. He is attempting to make sense out of suffering and to give a positive meaning to something which is experienced as decidedly negative. To a community caught in the throes of hostility and the possible threat of persecution, to a community strongly tempted to give up and return to easier, more acceptable ways, our homilist says: many before you have done it; Jesus has done it; the Father does this for your own good. Finally, he tells us that it hurts now but will benefit us in the end. The urgency of the homilist who seeks any means to convince is very evident here. It is also somewhat painful to witness. The arguments do not, in fact, convince; they are somewhat weak. The anxiety the preacher feels on behalf of the community pervades this section and witnesses to his own urgent need to encourage one another as the Day draws near (10:25). The section ends with a return to the image of the athlete. The homilist tells the members to "straighten up." Remove the things in your way so that you may continue.

V. THE CHRISTIAN RESPONSE.
12:14 – 13:19.

In the final section of Hebrews the homilist deals once again with the community's actual situation and with the danger the members face.

Hebrews 12:14-28 contains a magnificent portrayal of the Christian's glorious encounter with God in the heavenly Jerusalem. The new covenant encounter (12:22-24) is contrasted with the old covenant encounter (vss. 18-21) and both are enclosed within warnings against apostasy (14-17; 25-28). The section from 12:14-28 is really a summary of the homily which contains all of the major themes of Hebrews. Chapter 13 consists of a series of admonitions and a final exhortation: "Let us go forth!"

NO SECOND CHANCE.
12:14-17.

> ¹⁴Strive for peace with all men, and for the holiness without which no one will see the Lord. ¹⁵See to it that no one fail to obtain the grace of God; that no "root of bitterness" spring up and cause trouble, and by it the many become defiled; ¹⁶that no one be immoral or irreligious like Esau, who sold his birthright for a single meal. ¹⁷For you know that afterward, when he desired to inherit the blessing, he was rejected, for he found no chance to repent, though he sought it with tears.

The image of a race and of the fitness of the athlete disappears now and exhortation becomes a deadly warning.

Hebrews 12:14-17 contains a triple warning each more intense than the other. The structure of these verses helps to create the atmosphere of seriousness for each successive statement is longer and more detailed than the one which preceded. The first exhorts the members to actively pursue peace and to seek after holiness. Peace with all can refer to the situation in the community where undoubtedly there is less than perfect harmony. It can also refer to the ultimate eschatological peace, the gift of the Risen Lord wherein humankind and God are together in right relationship.

Holiness, or sanctification, is seen by the homilist as the ultimate goal. It was to achieve this sanctification that Jesus shared in our human existence and sacrificed himself. The exhortation to "seek holiness" indicates that the Christians have a part to play in their own salvation. What Jesus has done must be actualized in the life of each individual. The note of warning enters when we are reminded that without sanctification no one will see God. To see God, to enter the Holy Place, this is the result of the sanctification attained by Jesus. It is also that for which and from which one lives, according to our homilist. One can lose it, we are reminded.

The second phrase becomes an admonition: See to it that no one in the community falls from the grace of God. The homilist has previously warned against failing to enter God's rest in 4:1. The dynamic here is the same. Having portrayed the promise of God's rest which stood open to the believer, the members were warned not to lose that. The promise of salvation in the new covenant has been carefully and elaborately presented in chapters 8-10 and now the "Hebrews" are warned lest they fail to grasp it. They are also reminded to take care for each other, a responsibility stressed in 10:24-25.

They are to take care that no root of bitterness spring up and defile the community. The reference to a "root of bitterness" might lead us to envision acrimonious factions within the group. This is not the case, however. "Root of bitterness" is a citation of Deuteronomy 29:18 and refers to anyone who turns from worship of the true God to idolatry. Here the homilist warns those who would turn from true worship to false religious practices. He is concerned that rejection of the christian message by one member could lead to loss of the whole community.

This concern becomes more evident in the last warning. The story of Esau is recalled and is made to serve as an example of the fate in store for the apostate. Esau was Jacob's eldest son and possessed the special rights to inheritance that belonged to the first-born son. Genesis 26:27-34 relate that Esau, upon returning from hunting one day, sold his birthright to Jacob for some pottage. The story ends: "Thus Esau despised his birthright." (Gen 26:34). Later, when Esau sought to obtain his father's blessing, he found that Jacob had tricked his father into giving him the blessing instead of Esau (see Gen ch. 27). Esau, then, lost the two most important things that were his by birth.

Our homilist uses these two stories to make a startling point. Because Esau sold his birthright for so little ("a single meal") he stands as model of the apostate. He rejected what was given to him. Even more seriously, when Esau tried to repent he couldn't. In this text the homilist states what he has previously suggested: for the apostate there is no second repentance.

The question of second repentance in Hebrews has long been a source of debate. Many attempts have been made to mitigate the harsh statements or to interpret them "psychologically" and say the sinner's heart became so hardened that he was psychologically incapable of repentance. All such attempts fail. The homilist does say, here, in 6:4-8 and in 10:26-31, that there is *no* second chance for one guilty of apostasy.

In order to understand this, it is important to recognize why the author says this. We have seen over and over again that repetition is symbolic of imperfection in Hebrews. Christ died *once*, he made one perfect sacrifice. To say a second is possible is to deny the efficacy of the first, just as the promise of a second covenant proves that the first was faulty. In the same way, entrance into Christianity cannot be repeated. Hebrews 6:4-5 stresses this fact. As Christ died once, so too one becomes Christian *once*. Therefore, if one knowingly rejects that conversion, there is nothing to be done. To repeat this would imply a repetition of the sacrifice which made it possible and "there is no longer any offering for sin" (10:18).

We must also remember that Hebrews is not a doctrinal treatise nor is it an official, formal statement. It is a *homily* and homilies are intended to proclaim, to call to conversion, to exhort and to motivate. The language of a homily is frequently emotional and is sometimes extreme. Such is the case in Hebrews. The unknown homilist addresses a community facing temptation, temptation to turn back and reject what is theirs. They stand to throw away *their* birthright. The homilist will do anything to prevent this. He portrays the Christ-event in all its magnificence, he calls his people to the hope that is theirs, he frightens them by showing what they stand to lose.

Further, the eschatological perspective of Hebrews is important. For our homilist, another final drama must take place before all is consummated. Jesus will come a second time (9:28), the Day is fast approaching (10:25), all creation will be shaken "yet once more" (12:26). The final judgment is on the horizon and its approach adds great urgency to the message. The Day is coming soon and there will not be time to change things, nor is there time to debate the matter!

Finally, we must be aware of what the homilist does *not* say. He does not say anyone has committed apostasy, nor that any sin other than apostasy cannot be repented. He sees his community in a very dangerous situation and warns them about what *could* be and not what *is*.

THE PROMISE RECEIVED.
12:18-24.

> [18]For you have not come to what may be touched, a blazing fire, and darkness, and gloom, and a tempest, [19]and the sound of a trumpet, and a voice whose words

> made the hearers entreat that no further messages be spoken to them. 20For they could not endure the order that was given, "If even a beast touches the mountain, it shall be stoned." 21Indeed, so terrifying was the sight that Moses said, "I tremble with fear." 22But you have come to Mount Zion and to the city of the living God, the heavenly Jerusalem, and to innumerable angels in festal gathering, 23and to the assembly of the first-born who are enrolled in heaven, and to a judge who is God of all, and to the spirits of just men made perfect, 24and to Jesus, the mediator of a new covenant, and to the sprinkled blood that speaks more graciously than the blood of Abel.

What *is*, is portrayed in the magnificent text of 12:18-24. This text is a summary of the entire homily. By means of a detailed comparison, it portrays christian existence in all its grace and splendor. The homilist begins by depicting the great old covenant event: the encounter at Sinai. It was at Sinai that the first covenant was given and that Israel met her God. The Sinai event became the touchstone for all later events and the memory of Sinai allowed Israel to continue toward the promised goal. The homilist combines several Old Testament accounts of this event to recreate not only the fact of Sinai but the atmosphere and the emotions of Sinai. He goes beyond this, however, and by editing the Old Testament texts and additions of his own, interprets Sinai and interprets it negatively.

The elements such as fire, thunder, gloom, sound of a trumpet are all in the Old Testament accounts and are standard ways of speaking of the presence of God. Further, the people did ask Moses to go up the mountain and receive God's message, and there was a command not to let even an animal approach the holy mountain. The homilist, however, began the description by saying the "Hebrews" have not come to what can be touched, and in so doing, he has characterized the whole event as a palpable, external one. He has also added a reference to Moses. The Old Testament says nothing of Moses' fear. He climbed Sinai and encountered God with complete impunity. Here, however, we are told that Moses, mediator of the old covenant, trembled at the "terrifying sight." There is no reference to a message from God, only to a voice whose words frightened the people. There is, in fact, no real encounter. Sinai, the old covenant, is presented here as non-encounter, even the mediator did not really meet God.

Here is the homilist's final judgment on the old covenant: it was ineffectual; it kept the people from God rather than leading them to him. All that has been said about the old covenant law, cult, priesthood, sacrifice, institutions is recalled here and summarized. Even at Sinai it was impossible for anyone to approach God.

All is different now, however. Instead of Sinai, where God appeared, the Christians have come to Mount Zion, the place where, according to tradition, God dwells. They have come to the city of the living God, the heavenly Jerusalem. This is the city which God has prepared for the faithful, the one desired but not reached by Abraham and Sarah (11:13-16). The Christians join with innumerable angels in festal gathering. They are not surrounded by fearsome elements and too frightened to come before God; they are, rather, in company with all those who stand before God in praise and joy. Together with the angels are all of those who waited for the perfect sacrifice and the destruction of the barrier of sin, those who "apart from us could not be made perfect" (11:40). These are the first-born who, in contrast to Esau, have inherited the promise. They are the just who have been made perfect. All who lived by faith, who remained faithful to the promises of God, are now joined together in joy and praise!

They are not alone, however. They stand before God who is judge. Two things must be said here. First, the new covenant encounter is truly encounter, the Christians do not hear trumpets, see storms and gloom, they meet God. The veil is removed, all now enter the Holy Place, all stand before their God. Second, the note of urgency in Hebrews is not lost even here. God is judge. The Christians must still answer for their lives.

They also come to Jesus, mediator of the new covenant, and to the sprinkled blood. Here we are reminded of all that has been said of the new, better covenant established in Jesus' blood. With these two phrases the homilist sums up all that he has told us of the sacrifice of Jesus and of its meaning in our lives. This blood speaks, he says, and it speaks more graciously than Abel's. In 11:4 the homilist referred to Abel's blood which, according to the Old Testament, cries for vengeance. Jesus' blood, shed for us, cries out in mercy and forgiveness. It speaks the message of salvation.

The "Hebrews," then, have not approached a fearful sight where they do not really meet God. They have come to the dwelling place of this God where they join with all the faithful and with the angels. They are in the presence of God and of his Son, the mediator. They do not fear but are joyful. They do not hear of vengeance but of mercy. This joy-filled encounter is the inheritance, the promise, the culmination of the new covenant, the reality established in the sacrifice of Jesus. This is the lot and portion of the Christian. This is, finally, what the Christian is in danger of rejecting.

THE FINAL WARNING.
12:25-29.

> 25 See that you do not refuse him who is speaking. For if they did not escape when they refused him who warned them on earth, much less shall we escape if we reject him who warns from heaven. 26 His voice then shook the earth; but now he has promised, "Yet once more I will shake not only the earth but also the heaven." 27 This phrase, "Yet once more," indicates the removal of what is shaken, as of what has been made, in order that what cannot be shaken may remain. 28 Therefore let us be grateful for receiving a kingdom that cannot be shaken, and thus let us offer to God acceptable worship, with reverence and awe; 29 for our God is a consuming fire.

The danger involved in rejecting this gift is stressed in the final warning of the homily. In this warning, the homilist develops the idea of speaking—and of turning from the one who speaks. It is worth noting that the spoken word is stressed here just as it was in the beginning of Hebrews. The community is urged to *hear* and to pay heed to what they hear.

In 12:25-29 one last old covenant/new covenant comparison is made, this time in terms of the punishment given to those who turn from the word of God. The homilist picks up the reference to speaking in verse 24 and develops it into a full-blown warning. "Do not reject the one who speaks," we are told. "The old covenant people did reject and you know what happened to them!" The reference here is to Sinai as well as to the event in the wilderness described in Hebrews 3:17 – 4:7. The Israelites hardened their hearts, did not listen to the voice of God and were thus refused entry into the promised land and into the rest of God. If such a fate met them, how much worse a fate is in store for us if we reject so much greater a message.

The message is now given, by means of a citation of the prophet Haggai. Referring to the Sinai event, the homilist recalls that the voice of God shook the whole earth then, but *now*, God has spoken one last unchangeable word. He has promised that both heaven and earth will be shaken. The homilist has rearranged the original text (Haggai 2:6) somewhat in order to stress the fact that the heavens will also be shaken. For some, this is yet another indication that Hebrews reflects a dualistic mentality and that our homilist sees existence in terms of a heavenly (eternal, non-physical)/earthly (temporal, physical) dichotomy.

The christian encounter takes place in the heavenly Jerusalem, whereas the old covenant non-encounter was characterized by "what may be touched" (12:18). There is a heavenly/earthly comparison here, as there was in chapter 8 with its discussion of the true tent, made by the Lord (8:2), and in chapter 11 concerning the better country, "a heavenly one" (11:16). The old covenant, in all its aspects, was an earthly one. It was incapable of leading its members to the presence of God. The new covenant, on the other hand, is heavenly. Its members stand before God and the Son of God seated at the right hand of God's throne. It must be remembered, however, that the idea of heaven as the dwelling place of God was a common one in the Judaic tradition. The heavenly Jerusalem was frequently seen to be the city where God dwelled, the city that would be made visible at the end of time. Our homilist is probably combining several strands of thought and expression here in order to make his point: citizenship in the heavenly Jerusalem does not mean automatic salvation. One must remain faithful and persevere in holiness.

In verse 27 a single phrase of the Haggai quotation is commented upon. This phrase, "yet once more," is a natural one for our homilist to choose. We have seen how important the one-time character of the Christ-event is for him. There is another, future one-time event. This event, the shaking of heaven and earth, will result in the removal of what can be shaken, "as of what has been made." Here the homilist recalls the beginning of the homily (1:10-12) where the citation of Psalm 102:25-27 states that although the created world will pass away, God remains forever. In 12:27 the idea concerns more the community itself. Those Christians who can be shaken will not endure. They will not survive the last judgment.

The community's response to this warning is gratitude and worship. Having been given the unshakeable kingdom, they are to be grateful, to have grace (see 12:15 "that no one fail to obtain the grace of God") and thus offer acceptable worship. This worship is to be done with reverence and great awe (the Greek word here can also mean "fear"). The homilist ends the warning and, in a sense, the homily itself, on a somber note. He quotes Deuteronomy 4:24 and reminds his people of the One before whom they stand. The mighty God, the God of judgment, "a consuming fire." Christianity is a great gift, great joy; it is also great risk.

CONCLUDING ADMONITIONS.
13:1-9.

13 Let brotherly love continue. ²Do not neglect to show hospitality to strangers, for thereby some have entertained angels unawares. ³Remember those who are in prison, as though in prison with them; and those who are ill-treated, since you also are in the body. ⁴Let marriage be held in honor among all, and let the marriage bed be undefiled; for God will judge the immoral and adulterous. ⁵Keep your life free from love of money, and be content with what you have; for he has said, "I will never fail you nor forsake you." ⁶Hence we can confidently say,

"The Lord is my helper,
I will not be afraid;
what can man do to me?"

⁷Remember your leaders, those who spoke to you the word of God; consider the outcome of their life, and imitate their faith. ⁸Jesus Christ is the same yesterday and today and for ever. ⁹Do not be led away by diverse and strange teachings; for it is well that the heart be strengthened by grace, not by foods, which have not benefited their adherents.

The tone of the homily changes radically now and several brief admonitions follow. This change is so drastic that many scholars have concluded that chapter 13 was not originally part of Hebrews and that it was added later by a different person. At first reading this position appears to be a valid one. Nowhere else in Hebrews do we find admonitions concerning hospitality, marriage, financial affairs or relationship to leaders. The style of the language also differs markedly. Instead of carefully constructed, elaborately conceived imagery, we have short, disconnected sentences jumping from one idea to another almost at random. There are, however, some sections of chapter 13 which so clearly echo the thought and style of our homilist that this author, at least, is convinced that the chapter is an integral part of Hebrews.

Verses 1-7 contain reminders that cover all aspects of the Christian's daily life. They begin abruptly with "let brotherly love continue" (13:1). With the warning of 12:25-29, the great point has been made. One can almost hear the homilist's voice drop as he instructs his sisters and brothers on their daily lives. They must care for each other and always show hospitality. Hospitality was a very important aspect of life in a culture without motels, advance registration or travel agents. The mention of entertaining angels refers to the many Old Testament accounts where such things did happen. The most well-known is the delightful account in Genesis 18:1-15 where Abraham and Sarah were hospitable to three angels.

The second admonition concerns those in prison or who are ill-treated. Perhaps the homilist refers to those in the community who are suffering the beginnings of persecution, such as were mentioned in 10:32-34. He next speaks of marriage and of the evil of adultery. The sanctity of marriage was of urgent concern to early Christianity as the statements in Corinthians (ch. 7), Galatians (ch. 5), and Ephesians (ch. 5) show. The "Hebrews" are not to seek for greater financial success but are to be content with what they have. A pertinent reminder in our twentieth century consumer society! The homilist recalls for the community that God is their support and he will take care of them. He cites Deuteronomy 31:6 and Psalm 118:6 to prove this.

The members are exhorted to remember and to imitate their leaders. These "leaders" are those who first spoke the Good News to the community (see 2:3). They had remained faithful to the word of God and it is this fidelity that the "Hebrews" are to imitate. There is one more who is to be imitated: Jesus Christ. He is the one who is always the same, who "lives to make intercession for us" (7:25). This praise of Jesus Christ has the ring of a liturgical credo, and perhaps our homilist repeats here a statement known by his community.

LET US GO FORTH.
13:10-19.

> [10]We have an altar from which those who serve the tent have no right to eat. [11]For the bodies of those animals whose blood is brought into the sanctuary by the high priest as a sacrifice for sin are burned outside the camp. [12]So Jesus also suffered outside the gate in order to sanctify the people through his own blood. [13]Therefore let us go forth to him outside the camp, and bear the abuse he endured. [14]For here we have no lasting city, but we seek the city which is to come. [15]Through him then let us continually offer up a sacrifice of praise to God, that is, the fruit of lips that acknowledge his name. [16]Do not neglect to do good and to share what you have, for such sacrifices are pleasing to God.
>
> [17]Obey your leaders and submit to them; for they are keeping watch over your souls, as men who will have to give account. Let them do this joyfully, and not sadly, for that would be of no advantage to you.
>
> [18]Pray for us, for we are sure that we have a clear conscience, desiring to act honorably in all things. [19]I urge you the more earnestly to do this in order that I may be restored to you the sooner.

The community is warned about "diverse and strange teachings," which apparently dealt with dietary regulations. One of the great problems for early Christianity was the observance or non-observance of Judaic dietary laws. Paul spends a great deal of time discussing the issue in 1 Corinthians 8 and 10, for example. At issue is not the question of what one eats but rather a return to observance of Judaic law. The law is not seen as evil nor—by any means—is Judaism. What *is* wrong is the rejection of Christianity.

The reference to foods leads to a discussion of the respective sacrifices and here we hear clear echoes of our homilist's own thoughts. The Christians have an altar to which unbelievers are denied access. We are not to think of an actual physical altar here, such as we have in our contemporary churches. Rather, the "altar" is the sacrifice of Jesus himself. The homilist is not comparing the physical make-up of the respective "churches," but rather the significance of the respective sacrifices themselves.

Once more an element of the Day of Atonement ritual is used as ground for comparison. The animals used for sacrifice in that ceremony had to be completely destroyed. After the blood was shed, the bodies were taken outside of the camp, away from the sacred place. This fact leads to a recollection that Jesus was taken outside the city of Jerusalem to be crucified. He was the true sacrificial victim whose blood sanctified the people.

The Christians are to join him. They are to leave the "sacred" ground and go to the unholy, the place where Christ is. The exhortation in 13:13, "Let us go forth. . ." is the key to Hebrews. It is what our homilist has said repeatedly. It is risky business to go forth, to leave the security of the accepted, the known, the conventionally holy. But, we are told, that is where Jesus is. . . out there, outside the camp. Let us go to him, even if it means sharing his shame. Once again the city is spoken of, the lasting city, the city of God. It is not "here" but rather in the future. Already members of the heavenly Jerusalem, the Christians must still wait for its full and final revelation. In the meantime they must offer the sacrifice of the new covenant. The acceptable sacrifice now is to be seen in the lives of the believers. They are to praise God, do good, share with each other. A succinct definition of the life of faith!

Once again the leaders are mentioned. This time it is the present leaders who are spoken of. While the members are to obey them and make them joyful, we are not to envision a structured, hierarchical institution here. These leaders were those who spoke God's word and were accepted by the community for their wisdom and their goodness. Verses 18-19 urge the community to pray for the homilist himself. He asks this especially so that he "may be restored" to them. This phrase is very Pauline, for Paul often spoke of his travel plans and of his desire to return to the communities he had founded. This verse also implies that the homilist is no longer with his community. Verses 19 and 22-25 are clearly additions to the homily, added when it was written and circulated to the communities.

CONCLUSION:
A FINAL BLESSING
13:20-25.

> [20]Now may the God of peace who brought again from the dead our Lord Jesus, the great shepherd of the sheep, by the blood of the eternal covenant, [21]equip you with everything good that you may do his will, working in you that which is pleasing in his sight, through Jesus Christ; to whom be glory for ever and ever. Amen.
>
> [22]I appeal to you, brethren, bear with my word of exhortation, for I have written to you briefly. [23]You should understand that our brother Timothy has been released, with whom I shall see you if he comes soon. [24]Greet all your leaders and all the saints. Those who come from Italy send you greetings. [25]Grace be with all of you. Amen.

Verses 20-21 contain a final prayer for the community. The presence of such prayers is another element in the Pauline epistles (see, for example Rom 16:25-27, Phil 4:19-20). The content is consonant with Hebrews and draws together many major themes of the homily. It is a magnificent ending to a homily unlike any other. The prayer has two motifs. It begins by recalling what God (the God of peace) has done in Christ. God has brought Jesus from the dead much as Moses, the shepherd of his flock, was brought up out of the sea (Is 63:11). The title "Lord Jesus" is unique here and draws together the earthly ministry of Jesus and his being made Lord in resurrection. The phrase "blood of the eternal covenant" recalls the sacrifice of Jesus and the new eternal order established in that sacrifice.

The second section of the invocation deals with the community. God is asked to equip them with all that is necessary to achieve the goal: "that you may do his will." One is reminded of the characterization of Jesus' sacrifice as obedience to God's will in 10:5-9. One is also reminded to take courage, for the same God who has raised Jesus will be at work in us, making us pleasing to him. Hebrews ends as it began; directing the eyes of the community to the mighty God who saves.

Verses 22-25 are an addendum, a postscript added when the homily was sent to other communities. They are significant for three reasons. In verse 22 the homilist defines Hebrews as a "word of exhortation." This definition is an apt one, for Hebrews is truly a word which calls the community forth out of their fears and temptations and urges them to courageous fidelity in face of the great risk that is faith in Jesus. Further, the name of Timothy is used. Some have seen this as an indication that Hebrews is a Pauline epistle. Timothy was well-known by *many* christian communities, however, and a reference to his condition does not allow us to conclude that Paul has written these words. Finally, those of Italy are mentioned. This reference tempts us to presume that Hebrews originated in Italy. The Greek is ambiguous here, however, and the phrase can refer either to those in Italy or those outside of Italy, an exiled community perhaps. The origin of Hebrews remains a mystery to us, as do the name of the homilist and the real name of the "Hebrews."

What is hopefully no longer a mystery is the message of Hebrews. In a post-Vatican II church, a post-christian age, in face of an often terrifying future, the cry of the unknown homilist touches the depths of our hearts and fills them with longing, with courage.

Come, my sisters, my brothers, let us go forth!

FOR FURTHER READING

1. English Language

Bruce, F. F., *The Epistle to the Hebrews: The English Text with Introduction, Exposition and Notes*. The New International Commentary on the New Testament (Grand Rapids: Wm. B. Eerdmans Publishing Co., 1964).
  This is the best of the contemporary English language commentaries. It displays solid scholarship and is well-written.

Buchanan, G. W., *To the Hebrews: Translation, Comment and Conclusions*. The Anchor Bible 36 (New York: Doubleday and Co., 1972).
  This commentary is interesting and readable. Its conclusions, while difficult to accept, are nonetheless original and thought-provoking.

Cody, A., 'Hebrews' in Fuller, R. C. (ed.), *A New Catholic Commentary on Holy Scripture* (London: Nelson, 1969).
  A brief commentary that is clear and helpful.

Davies, J. H., *A Letter to the Hebrews*. The Cambridge Bible Commentary on the New English Bible (Cambridge: Cambridge University Press, 1967).
  This brief commentary provides a very fine introduction to Hebrews. It is clear and succinct.

Fuller, Reginald, et al., *Hebrews, James, 1 and 2 Peter, Jude, Revelation*. Proclamation commentaries (Philadelphia: Fortress Press, 1977).
  A masterful presentation of the major questions about Hebrews. . . in 27 pages!

Moffatt, J., *A Critical and Exegetical Commentary on the Epistle to the Hebrews*. The International Critical Commentary 8 (Edinburgh: T. & T. Clarke, 1924).
  The classic English commentary. While it is now somewhat dated, its study of the Greek text and the background information it provides make it an invaluable tool for the student of Hebrews.

Montefiore, H. W., *The Epistle to the Hebrews*. Black's New Testament Commentaries (London: A. & C. Black, 1964).
A solid and readable commentary which gives a real feeling for this epistle.

2. French and German Works

It must be noted that the majority of important works on Hebrews are in languages other than English. Three of these must be mentioned since they have been influential in the formation of my own understanding of Hebrews.

Michel, O., *Der Brief an die Hebräer: Übersetzt und Erklärt*. Kritischexegetischer Kommentar über das Neue Testament begründet von H. A.W. Meyer, 13 (Göttingen: Vandenhoeck & Ruprecht: 12th ed., 1966).
Michel's commentary is a brilliantly balanced and delicately nuanced exposition of all aspects of Hebrews.

Spicq, C., *L'Épître aux Hébreux*, 2 vols. Etudes Bibliques (Paris: J. Gabalda et Cie., 1952-53).
The most famous of commentaries on Hebrews, it remains unsurpassed for its wealth of information, voluminous bibliography, and detailed exegesis.

Vanhoye, A., *La Structure Littéraire de l'Épître aux Hébreux*. Studia Neotestamentica 1 (Paris and Bruges: Desclée de Brouwer, 1976).
Vanhoye's minutely detailed study of the highly-developed structure of Hebrews has led many to a clearer insight into the way Hebrews 'works.'